W9-DGL-796

FLORIDA STATE
UNIVERSITY LIBRARIES

MAR 27 1995

TALLAHASSEE, FLORIDA

Labor Markets and Integrating National Economies

Integrating National Economies: Promise and Pitfalls

F. M. Scherer (Harvard University)
Competition Policies for an Integrated World Economy

Richard R. Nelson (Columbia University) and Sylvia Ostry (University of Toronto)
'High-Tech' Industrial Policies: Conflict and Cooperation

Alan O. Sykes (University of Chicago)
Product Standards for Internationally Integrated Goods Markets

Mitsuhiro Fukao (Bank of Japan)
Financial Integration, Corporate Governance, and the Performance of Multinational Companies

Richard J. Herring (University of Pennsylvania) and Robert E. Litan
(Department of Justice/Brookings Institution)
Financial Regulation in a Global Economy

Ronald G. Ehrenberg (Cornell University)
Labor Markets and Integrating National Economies

Susan M. Collins (Brookings Institution/Georgetown University)
Distributive Issues: A Constraint on Global Integration

Robert Z. Lawrence (Harvard University)
Regionalism, Multilateralism, and Deeper Integration

Anne O. Krueger (Stanford University)
Trade Policies and Developing Nations

Richard N. Cooper (Harvard University)
Environment and Resource Policies for the World Economy

Ralph C. Bryant (Brookings Institution)
International Coordination of National Stabilization Policies

Vito Tanzi (International Monetary Fund)
Taxation in an Integrating World

Barry Eichengreen (University of California, Berkeley)
International Monetary Arrangements for the 21st Century

Miles Kahler (University of California, San Diego)
International Institutions and the Political Economy of Integration

Barry Bosworth (Brookings Institution) and Gur Ofer (Hebrew University)
Reforming Planned Economies in an Integrating World Economy

Robert L. Paarlberg (Wellesley College/Harvard University)
Leadership Abroad Begins at Home: U.S. Foreign Economic Policy after the Cold War

William Wallace (St. Antony's College, Oxford University)
Regional Integration: The West European Experience

Akihiko Tanaka (Institute of Oriental Culture, University of Tokyo)
The Politics of Deeper Integration: National Attitudes and Policies in Japan

Peter Rutland (Wesleyan University)
Russia, Eurasia, and the Global Economy

Susan L. Shirk (University of California, San Diego)
How China Opened Its Door: The Political Success of the PRC's Foreign Trade and Investment Reform

Stephan Haggard (University of California, San Diego)
Developing Nations and the Politics of Global Integration

Ronald G. Ehrenberg

Labor Markets and Integrating National Economies

THE BROOKINGS INSTITUTION
Washington, D.C.

HD
5706
E38
1994

Copyright © 1994
THE BROOKINGS INSTITUTION
1775 Massachusetts Avenue, N. W., Washington, D.C. 20036

All rights reserved

Library of Congress Cataloging-in-Publication data:
Ehrenberg, Ronald G.
Labor markets and integrating national economies/Ronald G. Ehrenberg
p. cm. — (Integrating national economies)
Includes bibliographical references and index.
ISBN 0-8157-2256-7 (cl) — ISBN 0-8157-2257-5 (pa)
1. Labor market.   2. Labor policy—International cooperation.
3. International economic integration.   4. Labor market—European
Economic Community countries.   5. Labor policy—European Economic
Community countries.   6. Europe—Economic integration.
I. Title.   II. Series.
HD5706.E38   1994
331. 12—dc20   94-14187
                                                           CIP
                                                           r94

9 8 7 6 5 4 3 2 1

The paper used in this publication meets the minimum requirements of
American National Standard for Information Sciences—Permanence of Paper
for Printed Library Materials, ANSI Z39.48-1984

Typeset in Plantin

Composition by Princeton Editorial Associates
Princeton, New Jersey

Printed by R. R. Donnelley and Sons Co.
Harrisonburg, Virginia

ℬ THE BROOKINGS INSTITUTION

The Brookings Institution is an independent organization devoted to nonpartisan research, education, and publication in economics, government, foreign policy, and the social sciences generally. Its principal purposes are to aid in the development of sound public policies and to promote public understanding of issues of national importance.

The Institution was founded on December 8, 1927, to merge the activities of the Institute for Government Research, founded in 1916, the Institute of Economics, founded in 1922, and the Robert Brookings Graduate School of Economics and Government, founded in 1924.

The Board of Trustees is responsible for the general administration of the Institution, while the immediate direction of the policies, program, and staff is vested in the President, assisted by an advisory committee of the officers and staff. The by-laws of the Institution state: "It is the function of the Trustees to make possible the conduct of scientific research, and publication, under the most favorable conditions, and to safeguard the independence of the research staff in the pursuit of their studies and in the publication of the results of such studies. It is not a part of their function to determine, control, or influence the conduct of particular investigations or the conclusions reached."

The President bears final responsibility for the decision to publish a manuscript as a Brookings book. In reaching his judgment on the competence, accuracy, and objectivity of each study, the President is advised by the director of the appropriate research program and weighs the views of a panel of expert outside readers who report to him in confidence on the quality of the work. Publication of a work signifies that it is deemed a competent treatment worthy of public consideration but does not imply endorsement of conclusions or recommendations.

The Institution maintains its position of neutrality on issues of public policy in order to safeguard the intellectual freedom of the staff. Hence interpretations or conclusions in Brookings publications should be understood to be solely those of the authors and should not be attributed to the Institution, to its trustees, officers, or other staff members, or to the organizations that support its research.

Board of Trustees

James A. Johnson
Chairman

Leonard Abramson
Ronald J. Arnault
Rex J. Bates
A. W. Clausen
John L. Clendenin
D. Ronald Daniel
Walter Y. Elisha
Stephen Friedman

William H. Gray III
Vartan Gregorian
Teresa Heinz
Samuel Hellman
Warren Hellman
Thomas W. Jones
Vernon E. Jordan, Jr.
James A. Joseph
Breene M. Kerr
Thomas G. Labrecque
Donald F. McHenry

Bruce K. MacLaury
David O. Maxwell
Constance Berry Newman
Maconda Brown O'Connor
Samuel Pisar
David Rockefeller, Jr.
Michael P. Schulhof
Robert H. Smith
John D. Zeglis
Ezra K. Zilkha

Honorary Trustees

Elizabeth E. Bailey
Vincent M. Barnett, Jr.
Barton M. Biggs
Louis W. Cabot
Edward W. Carter
Frank T. Cary
William T. Coleman, Jr.
Kenneth W. Dam
Bruce B. Dayton
Douglas Dillon
Charles W. Duncan, Jr.
Robert F. Erburu

Robert D. Haas
Andrew Heiskell
Roger W. Heyns
Roy M. Huffington
Nannerl O. Keohane
James T. Lynn
William McC. Martin, Jr.
Robert S. McNamara
Mary Patterson McPherson
Arjay Miller
Donald S. Perkins

J. Woodward Redmond
Charles W. Robinson
James D. Robinson III
Howard D. Samuel
B. Francis Saul II
Ralph S. Saul
Henry B. Schacht
Gerard C. Smith
Robert Brookings Smith
Morris Tanenbaum
John C. Whitehead
James D. Wolfensohn

Foreword

ECONOMIES around the world are becoming increasingly integrated. The past year saw the passage of the North American Free Trade Act and the successful completion of a round of negotiations under the General Agreement on Tariffs and Trade. These forms of international economic integration promote trade and capital mobility. Other forms, such as those being pursued by the European Community nations, also promote the mobility of workers across national boundaries.

In this book, part of the Brookings series Integrating National Economies: Promise and Pitfalls, Ronald Ehrenberg examines how labor market institutions and policies influence trade flows, capital mobility, and labor mobility and the pace at which international economic integration proceeds. He also discusses the pressures to change some labor market institutions and policies that arise from integration.

Ultimately, economic integration poses issues relating to trade-offs between efficiency and equity and to what each nation judges to be desirable levels of labor market standards and social protection. Ehrenberg argues that economic integration can take place between nations with very different levels of labor market standards and policies. However, he concludes that the desirability and political acceptability of proposals for increased integration may hinge on policies that facilitate adjustment, both within and across nations, as well as on some convergence of labor standards across nations. Put another way, the political process may allow the benefits from increased trade and labor-capital mobility to be fully achieved only if nations systematically develop ways to have some of their labor market policies converge.

Ronald G. Ehrenberg is the Irving M. Ives Professor of Industrial and Labor Relations and Economics at Cornell University and a research associate at the National Bureau of Economic Research. He is grateful to

Richard Freeman and Stephen Nickell for providing detailed comments on both an initial outline and an early draft. He is also grateful to many others in the United States and around the world who offered substantive comments and assistance. He especially wishes to thank Henry J. Aaron, Ralph C. Bryant, Gary Burtless, Susan M. Collins, Gary Fields, Robert Flanagan, Daniel Hamermesh, Robert Hebdon, James Jacobs, Peter Katzenstein, Anne O. Krueger, Robert Z. Lawrence, John Martin, Daniel Mitchell, Olivia Mitchell, Peter Scherer, Solomon Polachek, Jules Theeuwes, Lowell Turner, Wayne Vroman, and John Windmuller.

Ehrenberg is also indebted to Shirley Harper, retired director of the Martin P. Catherwood Library at Cornell University's School of Industrial and Labor Relations, who, along with her colleagues, built up and maintained one of the world's leading collections of materials dealing with all aspects of labor markets. At Cornell, Patricia Dickerson prepared repeated drafts of the text and tables. At Brookings, Caroline Lalire edited the manuscript, Laura Kelly verified it, and David Rossetti provided staff assistance. Princeton Editorial Associates prepared the index.

Funding for the project came from the Center for Global Partnership of the Japan Foundation, the Curry Fund, the Ford Foundation, the Korea Foundation, the Tokyo Club Foundation for Global Studies, the United States–Japan Foundation, and the Alex C. Walker Educational and Charitable Foundation. The author and Brookings are grateful for their support.

The views expressed in the study are those of the author and should not be ascribed to any of the persons or organizations acknowledged above, or to the trustees, officers, or staff members of the Brookings Institution.

BRUCE K. MACLAURY
President

June 1994
Washington, D.C.

*To Shirley Harper,
friend and colleague, who has made
both this book and so much other
social science research possible*

Contents

Tables

Figures

Preface to the Studies on Integrating National Economies

ECONOMIC interdependence among nations has increased sharply in the past half century. For example, while the value of total production of industrial countries increased at a rate of about 9 percent a year on average between 1964 and 1992, the value of the exports of those nations grew at an average rate of 12 percent, and lending and borrowing across national borders through banks surged upward even more rapidly at 23 percent a year. This international economic interdependence has contributed to significantly improved standards of living for most countries. Continuing international economic integration holds out the promise of further benefits. Yet the increasing sensitivity of national economies to events and policies originating abroad creates dilemmas and pitfalls if national policies and international cooperation are poorly managed.

The Brookings Project on Integrating National Economies, of which this study is a component, focuses on the interplay between two fundamental facts about the world at the end of the twentieth century. First, the world will continue for the foreseeable future to be organized politically into nation-states with sovereign governments. Second, increasing economic integration among nations will continue to erode differences among national economies and undermine the autonomy of national governments. The project explores the opportunities and tensions arising from these two facts.

Scholars from a variety of disciplines have produced twenty-one studies for the first phase of the project. Each study examines the heightened competition between national political sovereignty and increased cross-border economic integration. This preface identifies background themes and issues common to all the studies and provides a brief overview of the project as a whole.[1]

---

1. A complete list of authors and study titles is included at the beginning of this volume, facing the title page.

Increasing World Economic Integration

Two underlying sets of causes have led nations to become more closely intertwined. First, technological, social, and cultural changes have sharply reduced the effective economic distances among nations. Second, many of the government policies that traditionally inhibited cross-border transactions have been relaxed or even dismantled.

The same improvements in transportation and communications technology that make it much easier and cheaper for companies in New York to ship goods to California, for residents of Strasbourg to visit relatives in Marseilles, and for investors in Hokkaido to buy and sell shares on the Tokyo Stock Exchange facilitate trade, migration, and capital movements spanning nations and continents. The sharply reduced costs of moving goods, money, people, and information underlie the profound economic truth that technology has made the world markedly smaller.

New communications technology has been especially significant for financial activity. Computers, switching devices, and telecommunications satellites have slashed the cost of transmitting information internationally, of confirming transactions, and of paying for transactions. In the 1950s, for example, foreign exchange could be bought and sold only during conventional business hours in the initiating party's time zone. Such transactions can now be carried out instantaneously twenty-four hours a day. Large banks pass the management of their worldwide foreign-exchange positions around the globe from one branch to another, staying continuously ahead of the setting sun.

Such technological innovations have increased the knowledge of potentially profitable international exchanges and of economic opportunities abroad. Those developments, in turn, have changed consumers' and producers' tastes. Foreign goods, foreign vacations, foreign financial investments—virtually anything from other nations—have lost some of their exotic character.

Although technological change permits increased contact among nations, it would not have produced such dramatic effects if it had been countermanded by government policies. Governments have traditionally taxed goods moving in international trade, directly restricted imports and subsidized exports, and tried to limit international capital movements. Those policies erected "separation fences" at the borders of nations. From the perspective of private sector agents, separation fences imposed extra costs on cross-border transactions. They reduced trade and, in some cases, eliminated it. During the 1930s governments used such policies with particular zeal, a practice now believed to have deepened and lengthened the Great Depression.

After World War II, most national governments began—sometimes unilaterally, more often collaboratively—to lower their separation fences, to make them more permeable, or sometimes even to tear down parts of them. The multilateral negotiations under the auspices of the General Agreement on Trade and Tariffs (GATT)—for example, the Kennedy Round in the 1960s, the Tokyo Round in the 1970s, and most recently the protracted negotiations of the Uruguay Round, formally signed only in April 1994—stand out as the most prominent examples of fence lowering for trade in goods. Though contentious and marked by many compromises, the GATT negotiations are responsible for sharp reductions in at-the-border restrictions on trade in goods and services. After the mid-1980s a large number of developing countries moved unilaterally to reduce border barriers and to pursue outwardly oriented policies.

The lowering of fences for financial transactions began later and was less dramatic. Nonetheless, by the 1990s government restrictions on capital flows, especially among the industrial countries, were much less important and widespread than at the end of World War II and in the 1950s.

By shrinking the economic distances among nations, changes in technology would have progressively integrated the world economy even in the absence of reductions in governments' separation fences. Reductions in separation fences would have enhanced interdependence even without the technological innovations. Together, these two sets of evolutionary changes have reinforced each other and strikingly transformed the world economy.

Changes in the Government of Nations

Simultaneously with the transformation of the global economy, major changes have occurred in the world's political structure. First, the number of governmental decisionmaking units in the world has expanded markedly and political power has been diffused more broadly among them. Rising nationalism and, in some areas, heightened ethnic tensions have accompanied that increasing political pluralism.

The history of membership in international organizations documents the sharp growth in the number of independent states. For example, only 44 nations participated in the Bretton Woods conference of July 1944, which gave birth to the International Monetary Fund. But by the end of 1970, the IMF had 118 member nations. The number of members grew to 150 by the mid-1980s and to 178 by December 1993. Much of this growth reflects the collapse of colonial empires. Although many nations today are small and carry little individual weight in the global economy, their combined influence is considerable and their interests cannot be ignored as easily as they were in the past.

A second political trend, less visible but equally important, has been the gradual loss of the political and economic hegemony of the United States. Immediately after World War II, the United States by itself accounted for more than one-third of world production. By the early 1990s the U.S. share had fallen to about one-fifth. Concurrently, the political and economic influence of the European colonial powers continued to wane, and the economic significance of nations outside Europe and North America, such as Japan, Korea, Indonesia, China, Brazil, and Mexico, increased. A world in which economic power and influence are widely diffused has displaced a world in which one or a few nations effectively dominated international decisionmaking.

Turmoil and the prospect of fundamental change in the formerly centrally planned economies compose a third factor causing radical changes in world politics. During the era of central planning, governments in those nations tried to limit external influences on their economies. Now leaders in the formerly planned economies are trying to adopt reforms modeled on Western capitalist principles. To the extent that these efforts succeed, those nations will increase their economic involvement with the rest of the world. Political and economic alignments among the Western industrialized nations will be forced to adapt.

Governments and scholars have begun to assess these three trends, but their far-reaching ramifications will not be clear for decades.

Dilemmas for National Policies

Cross-border economic integration and national political sovereignty have increasingly come into conflict, leading to a growing mismatch between the economic and political structures of the world. The effective domains of economic markets have come to coincide less and less with national governmental jurisdictions.

When the separation fences at nations' borders were high, governments and citizens could sharply distinguish "international" from "domestic" policies. International policies dealt with at-the-border barriers, such as tariffs and quotas, or responded to events occurring abroad. In contrast, domestic policies were concerned with everything behind the nation's borders, such as competition and antitrust rules, corporate governance, product standards, worker safety, regulation and supervision of financial institutions, environmental protection, tax codes, and the government's budget. Domestic policies were regarded as matters about which nations were sovereign, to be determined by the preferences of the nation's citizens and its political institutions, without regard for effects on other nations.

As separation fences have been lowered and technological innovations have shrunk economic distances, a multitude of formerly neglected differences among nations' domestic policies have become exposed to international scrutiny. National governments and international negotiations must thus increasingly deal with "deeper"—behind-the-border—integration. For example, if country A permits companies to emit air and water pollutants whereas country B does not, companies that use pollution-generating methods of production will find it cheaper to produce in country A. Companies in country B that compete internationally with companies in country A are likely to complain that foreign competitors enjoy unfair advantages and to press for international pollution standards.

Deeper integration requires analysis of the economic and the political aspects of virtually all nonborder policies and practices. Such issues have already figured prominently in negotiations over the evolution of the European Community, over the Uruguay Round of GATT negotiations, over the North American Free Trade Agreement (NAFTA), and over the bilateral economic relationships between Japan and the United States. Future debates about behind-the-border policies will occur with increasing frequency and prove at least as complex and contentious as the past negotiations regarding at-the-border restrictions.

Tensions about deeper integration arise from three broad sources: cross-border spillovers, diminished national autonomy, and challenges to political sovereignty.

Cross-Border Spillovers

Some activities in one nation produce consequences that spill across borders and affect other nations. Illustrations of these spillovers abound. Given the impact of modern technology of banking and securities markets in creating interconnected networks, lax rules in one nation erode the ability of all other nations to enforce banking and securities rules and to deal with fraudulent transactions. Given the rapid diffusion of knowledge, science and technology policies in one nation generate knowledge that other nations can use without full payment. Labor market policies become matters of concern to other nations because workers migrate in search of work; policies in one nation can trigger migration that floods or starves labor markets elsewhere. When one nation dumps pollutants into the air or water that other nations breathe or drink, the matter goes beyond the unitary concern of the polluting nation and becomes a matter for international negotiation. Indeed, the hydrocarbons that are emitted into the atmosphere when individual nations burn coal for generating electricity contribute to global warming and are thereby a matter of concern for the entire world.

The tensions associated with cross-border spillovers can be especially vexing when national policies generate outcomes alleged to be competitively inequitable, as in the example in which country A permits companies to emit pollutants and country B does not. Or consider a situation in which country C requires commodities, whether produced at home or abroad, to meet certain design standards, justified for safety reasons. Foreign competitors may find it too expensive to meet these standards. In that event, the standards in C act very much like tariffs or quotas, effectively narrowing or even eliminating foreign competition for domestic producers. Citing examples of this sort, producers or governments in individual nations often complain that business is not conducted on a "level playing field." Typically, the complaining nation proposes that *other* nations adjust their policies to moderate or remove the competitive inequities.

Arguments for creating a level playing field are troublesome at best. International trade occurs precisely because of differences among nations—in resource endowments, labor skills, and consumer tastes. Nations specialize in producing goods and services in which they are relatively most efficient. In a fundamental sense, cross-border trade is valuable because the playing field is *not* level.

When David Ricardo first developed the theory of comparative advantage, he focused on differences among nations owing to climate or technology. But Ricardo could as easily have ascribed the productive differences to differing "social climates" as to physical or technological climates. Taking all "climatic" differences as given, the theory of comparative advantage argues that free trade among nations will maximize global welfare.

Taken to its logical extreme, the notion of leveling the playing field implies that nations should become homogeneous in all major respects. But that recommendation is unrealistic and even pernicious. Suppose country A decides that it is too poor to afford the costs of a clean environment, and will thus permit the production of goods that pollute local air and water supplies. Or suppose it concludes that it cannot afford stringent protections for worker safety. Country A will then argue that it is inappropriate for other nations to impute to country A the value they themselves place on a clean environment and safety standards (just as it would be inappropriate to impute the A valuations to the environment of other nations). The core of the idea of political sovereignty is to permit national residents to order their lives and property in accord with their own preferences.

Which perspective about differences among nations in behind-the-border policies is more compelling? Is country A merely exercising its national preferences and appropriately exploiting its comparative advantage in goods that are dirty or dangerous to produce? Or does a legitimate international problem exist that justifies pressure from other nations urging country A to accept changes in its policies (thus curbing its national sovereignty)? When national governments negotiate resolutions to such questions—trying to agree whether individual nations are legitimately exercising sovereign choices or, alternatively, engaging in behavior that is unfair or damaging to other nations—the dialogue is invariably contentious because the resolutions depend on the typically complex circumstances of the international spillovers and on the relative weights accorded to the interests of particular individuals and particular nations.

Diminished National Autonomy

As cross-border economic integration increases, governments experience greater difficulties in trying to control events within their borders. Those difficulties, summarized by the term *diminished autonomy*, are the second set of reasons why tensions arise from the competition between political sovereignty and economic integration.

For example, nations adjust monetary and fiscal policies to influence domestic inflation and employment. In setting these policies, smaller countries have always been somewhat constrained by foreign economic events and policies. Today, however, all nations are constrained, often severely. More than in the past, therefore, nations may be better able to achieve their economic goals if they work together collaboratively in adjusting their macroeconomic policies.

Diminished autonomy and cross-border spillovers can sometimes be allowed to persist without explicit international cooperation to deal with them. States in the United States adopt their own tax systems and set policies for assistance to poor single people without any formal cooperation or limitation. Market pressures operate to force a degree of de facto cooperation. If one state taxes corporations too heavily, it knows business will move elsewhere. (Those familiar with older debates about "fiscal federalism" within the United States and other nations will recognize the similarity between those issues and the emerging international debates about deeper integration of national economies.) Analogously, differences among nations in regulations, standards, policies, institutions, and even social and cultural preferences create economic incentives for a kind of arbitrage that erodes or eliminates the differences. Such pressures involve not only the conventional arbitrage that exploits price differentials (buying at one point in geographic space or time and selling at another) but also shifts in the location of production facilities and in the residence of factors of production.

In many other cases, however, cross-border spillovers, arbitrage pressures, and diminished effectiveness of national policies can produce unwanted consequences. In cases involving what economists call externalities (external economies and diseconomies), national governments may need to cooperate to promote mutual interests. For example, population growth, continued urbanization, and the more intensive exploitation of natural resources generate external diseconomies not only within but across national boundaries. External economies generated when benefits spill across national jurisdictions probably also increase in importance (for instance, the gains from basic research and from control of communicable diseases).

None of these situations is new, but technological change and the reduction of tariffs and quotas heighten their importance. When one nation produces goods (such as scientific research) or "bads" (such as pollution) that significantly affect other nations, individual governments acting sequentially and noncooperatively cannot deal effectively with the resulting issues. In the absence of explicit cooperation and political leadership, too few collective goods and too many collective bads will be supplied.

Challenges to Political Sovereignty

The pressures from cross-border economic integration sometimes even lead individuals or governments to challenge the core assumptions of national political sovereignty. Such challenges are a third source of tensions about deeper integration.

The existing world system of nation-states assumes that a nation's residents are free to follow their own values and to select their own political arrangements without interference from others. Similarly, property rights are allocated by nation. (The so-called global commons, such as outer space and the deep seabed, are the sole exceptions.) A nation is assumed to have the sovereign right to exploit its property in accordance with its own preferences and policies. Political sovereignty is thus analogous to the concept of consumer sovereignty (the presumption that the individual consumer best knows his or her own interests and should exercise them freely).

In times of war, some nations have had sovereignty wrested from them by force. In earlier eras, a handful of individuals or groups have questioned the premises of political sovereignty. With the profound increases in economic integration in recent decades, however, a larger number of individuals and groups—and occasionally even their national governments—have identified circumstances in which, it is claimed, some universal or international set of values should take precedence over the preferences or policies of particular nations.

Some groups seize on human-rights issues, for example, or what they deem to be egregiously inappropriate political arrangements in other nations. An especially prominent case occurred when citizens in many nations labeled the former apartheid policies of South Africa an affront to universal values and emphasized that the South African government was not legitimately representing the interests of a majority of South Africa's residents. Such views caused many national governments to apply economic sanctions against South Africa. Examples of value conflicts are not restricted to human rights, however. Groups focusing on environmental issues characterize tropical rain forests as the lungs of the world and the genetic repository for numerous species of plants and animals that are the heritage of all mankind. Such views lead Europeans, North Americans, or Japanese to challenge the timber-cutting policies of Brazilians and Indonesians. A recent controversy over tuna fishing with long drift nets that kill porpoises is yet another example. Environmentalists in the United States whose sensibilities were offended by the drowning of porpoises required U.S. boats at some additional expense to amend their fishing practices. The U.S. fishermen, complaining about imported tuna caught with less regard for porpoises, persuaded the U.S. government to ban such tuna imports (both direct imports from the countries in which the tuna is caught and indirect imports shipped via third countries). Mexico and Venezuela were the main countries affected by this ban; a GATT dispute panel sided with Mexico against the United States in the controversy, which further upset the U.S. environmental community.

A common feature of all such examples is the existence, real or alleged, of "psychological externalities" or "political failures." Those holding such views reject untrammeled political sovereignty for nation-states in deference to universal or non-national values. They wish to constrain the exercise of individual nations' sovereignties through international negotiations or, if necessary, by even stronger intervention.

The Management of International Convergence

In areas in which arbitrage pressures and cross-border spillovers are weak and psychological or political externalities are largely absent, national governments may encounter few problems with deeper integration. Diversity across nations may persist quite easily. But at the other extreme, arbitrage and spillovers in some areas may be so strong that they threaten to erode national diversity completely. Or psychological and political sensitivities may be asserted too powerfully to be ignored. Governments will then be confronted with serious tensions, and national policies and behaviors may eventually converge to common, worldwide patterns (for example, subject to internationally agreed norms or minimum standards). Eventual convergence across nations, if it occurs, could happen in a harmful way (national policies and practices being driven to a least common denominator with externalities ignored, in effect a "race to the bottom") or it could occur with mutually beneficial results ("survival of the fittest and the best").

Each study in this series addresses basic questions about the management of international convergence: if, when, and how national governments should intervene to try to influence the consequences of arbitrage pressures, cross-border spillovers, diminished autonomy, and the assertion of psychological or political externalities. A wide variety of responses is conceivable. We identify six, which should be regarded not as distinct categories but as ranges along a continuum.

National autonomy defines a situation at one end of the continuum in which national governments make decentralized decisions with little or no consultation and no explicit cooperation. This response represents political sovereignty at its strongest, undiluted by any international management of convergence.

Mutual recognition, like national autonomy, presumes decentralized decisions by national governments and relies on market competition to guide the process of international convergence. Mutual recognition, however, entails exchanges of information and consultations among governments to constrain the formation of national regulations and policies. As understood in discussions of economic integration within the European Community, moreover, mutual recognition entails an explicit acceptance by each member nation of the regulations, standards, and certification procedures of other members. For example, mutual recognition allows wine or liquor produced in any European Union country to be sold in all twelve member countries even if production standards in member countries differ. Doctors licensed in France are permitted to practice in Germany, and vice versa, even if licensing procedures in the two countries differ.

Governments may agree on rules that restrict their freedom to set policy or that promote gradual convergence in the structure of policy. As international consultations and monitoring of compliance with such rules become more important, this situation can be described as *monitored decentralization*. The Group of Seven finance ministers meetings, supplemented by the IMF's surveillance over exchange rate and macroeconomic policies, illustrate this approach to management.

Coordination goes further than mutual recognition and monitored decentralization in acknowledging convergence pressures. It is also more ambitious in promoting intergovernmental cooperation to deal with them. Coordination involves jointly designed mutual adjustments of national policies. In clear-cut cases of coordination, bargaining occurs and governments agree to behave differently from the ways they would have behaved without the agreement. Examples include the World Health Organization's procedures for controlling communicable diseases and the 1987 Montreal Protocol (to a 1985 framework convention) for the protection of stratospheric ozone by reducing emissions of chlorofluorocarbons.

Explicit harmonization, which requires still higher levels of intergovernmental cooperation, may require agreement on regional standards or world standards. Explicit harmonization typically entails still greater departures from decentralization in decisionmaking and still further strengthening of international institutions. The 1988 agreement among major central banks to set minimum standards for the required capital positions of commercial banks (reached through the Committee on Banking Regulations and Supervisory Practices at the Bank for International Settlements) is an example of partially harmonized regulations.

At the opposite end of the spectrum from national autonomy lies *federalist mutual governance*, which implies continuous bargaining and joint, centralized decisionmaking. To make federalist mutual governance work would require greatly strengthened supranational institutions. This end of the management spectrum, now relevant only as an analytical benchmark, is a possible outcome that can be imagined for the middle or late decades of the twenty-first century, possibly even sooner for regional groupings like the European Union.

Overview of the Brookings Project

Despite their growing importance, the issues of deeper economic integration and its competition with national political sovereignty were largely neglected in the 1980s. In 1992 the Brookings Institution initiated its project on Integrating National Economies to direct attention to these important questions.

In studying this topic, Brookings sought and received the cooperation of some of the world's leading economists, political scientists, foreign-policy specialists, and government officials, representing all regions of the world. Although some functional areas require a special focus on European, Japanese, and North American perspectives, at all junctures the goal was to include, in addition, the perspectives of developing nations and the formerly centrally planned economies.

The first phase of the project commissioned the twenty-one scholarly studies listed at the beginning of the book. One or two lead discussants, typically residents of parts of the world other than the area where the author resides, were asked to comment on each study.

Authors enjoyed substantial freedom to design their individual studies, taking due account of the overall themes and goals of the project. The guidelines for the studies requested that at least some of the analysis be carried out with a non-normative perspective. In effect, authors were asked to develop a "baseline" of what might happen in the absence of changed policies or further international cooperation. For their normative analyses, authors were asked to start with an agnostic posture that did not prejudge the net benefits or costs resulting from integration. The project organizers themselves had no presumption about whether national diversity is better or worse than international convergence or about what the individual studies should conclude regarding the desirability of increased integration. On the contrary, each author was asked to address the trade-offs in his or her issue area between diversity and convergence and to locate the area, currently and prospectively, on the spectrum of international management possibilities running between national autonomy through mutual recognition to coordination and explicit harmonization.

HENRY J. AARON   SUSAN M. COLLINS

RALPH C. BRYANT   ROBERT Z. LAWRENCE

Chapter 1

Introduction

THE international economy is becoming increasingly integrated. For example, between 1950 and 1988 exports as a share of gross domestic product rose from 9.4 to 15.2 percent in the world as a whole, from 3.5 to 6.7 percent in the United States and from 13.1 to 22.0 percent in the European Community (EC) nations.[1] Increased economic integration is due in part to reductions in transportation and communications costs, and in part to the growth of multilateral and bilateral arrangements that have reduced the tariff and nontariff barriers to trade and capital mobility. These include the General Agreement on Tariffs and Trade (GATT), the EC, and the United States–Canada Free Trade Agreement. The latter evolved, after much debate, into the North American Free Trade Agreement (NAFTA) and now includes Mexico.

Labor markets have a wide range of characteristics that influence trade flows and both capital and labor mobility. Hence these characteristics will also influence the pace at which economic integration proceeds. A major purpose of this book is to describe what these characteristics are and how they vary across nations, to indicate the lessons one can learn about how to reduce barriers to integration from the U.S. system of federal fiscalism and from the EC's experiences, and to suggest other potential policies to overcome barriers that may limit international economic integration. Because international economic integration may also create pressures to change some of the characteristics of labor markets, a second purpose of the book is to discuss some of those pressures.

1. Bloom and Brender (1993, table 18).

1

Pros and Cons of Increased Economic Integration

Policies to increase economic integration can take two forms. Some policies promote trade or capital mobility, or both. GATT is an example of this form, as is the recently passed NAFTA. Other policies also promote, or encourage, the mobility of labor, such as those developed by the EC that allow for free mobility of individuals across member nations and that require member nations to recognize professional credentials (for example, medical degrees) earned in other member nations.

Are both kinds of economic integration desirable? Trade is thought to increase economic efficiency by allowing nations to specialize in the production of those goods for which they have a comparative advantage and by allowing them to benefit from any economies of scale in production that may result from having a larger market for their goods. The mobility of capital is thought to allow capital-labor ratios to equalize across nations and thus to cause the equality of marginal productivities of capital (and labor) across nations, which should maximize total world output. Hence, in an efficiency sense, the case for free trade and capital mobility seems strong.

The discussion above ignores, however, the effect of trade and capital mobility on the income distributions in different countries. The passage of NAFTA, for example, may lead to reduced employment opportunities for Mexican agricultural workers and reduced employment opportunities for some U.S. manufacturing workers. To the extent that there is an identifiable group of "losers" in each country, domestic adjustment policies, such as retraining programs or income support programs, may help to guarantee widespread continued support for the legislation in both countries and to reduce changes in the distribution of income in each country that residents consider undesirable.

Of course, free mobility of labor would in some cases eliminate the need for countries to pursue domestic adjustment policies.[2] For example, if free mobility of labor were part of NAFTA (it currently is not), Mexican agricultural workers who became unemployed as a result of free trade could migrate to the United States to seek employment. But that would lead to another set of issues regarding how such a migration flow would influence both the distribution of earnings and infrastructure needs (such as schools) in the United States.

Both types of economic integration also lead to questions whether standards would be adequate and whether the level of labor market

---

2. Increased labor mobility may also reduce the amount of training employers are willing to finance for their employees and thus may create some efficiency losses. This possibility is discussed in chapter 3.

standards should be part of trade negotiations. Would increased free trade with poorer nations, like Mexico, cause the United States to reduce its occupational safety and health standards or its minimum wages in an effort to remain competitive with the poorer nations and their lower standards? Or rather than "tolerate" such a situation, should the United States agree to free trade with another nation only if the other nation raised its standards to a level close to ours? Or should free trade be accompanied by attempts to harmonize labor market standards across nations through a regional supranational body, such as the EC, or through a global organization?

Ultimately economic integration, either with or without free mobility of labor, raises issues relating to efficiency-equity trade-offs and to what each nation judges to be desirable levels of standards.[3] In the chapters that follow, I argue that economic integration *can* take place between nations with very different levels of labor market standards and policies. However, to be unambiguously judged as desirable, *and* to win political support, proposals for increased economic integration may require adjustment policies both within and across nations as well as the convergence of labor standards. Put another way, the political process may allow the benefits from increased trade and factor mobility to be fully achieved only if nations systematically develop methods to have some of their labor market policies converge. That is, in the parlance of the broader project of which this book is a part, for the benefits of increased trade and factor mobility to be fully achieved, internal political forces within each nation may lead to a form of deep integration of nation-states.

Outline of the Book

When one thinks of a market, one typically thinks of prices and quantities. Labor markets do have prices—namely, wages—and quantities—namely, levels of employment supplied and demanded. Labor markets are complicated phenomena, however, and have many other characteristics that influence either the benefits from increased trade and mobility or nations' ability to achieve greater economic integration. The next section of this chapter describes in general terms the characteristics of labor markets that are addressed in the book; the following one focuses on a stereotypical version of one characteristic, unemployment insurance to illustrate some of the issues that arise in a world with fixed exchange rates; and the last section extends the analysis by allowing exchange rates to vary. An appendix describing the EC follows.

3. Okun (1975).

Each of the five chapters that follow concentrates on one set of labor market characteristics. Data are drawn selectively from the United States, Canada, the Western European nations, Japan, and Mexico to show the variations in characteristics that currently exist across nations (or, in the case of the United States, across states). How in theory differences in characteristics would affect the likelihood of increased economic integration and how increased economic integration would affect the characteristics are discussed. Relevant empirical evidence is presented throughout.

Ultimately these chapters suggest four key issues, which I return to in the concluding chapter. First, do differences in levels of standards, benefits, or hours of work across nations imply that unfair competitive practices are being pursued and that these must be modified before increased economic integration can proceed? Second, do existing institutional arrangements limit labor mobility in an undesirable way? Third, given the potential distributional effects of increased economic integration, and the fact that sometimes its benefits are small for a large number of people (for example, lower prices for a variety of products), while its costs are large for a small number of people (for example, job loss for individuals in a few industries), are existing institutional arrangements sufficient to allow increased integration to occur? Finally, are there characteristics of labor markets that, if changed because of pressures for increased economic integration, may lead to efficiency losses?

The final chapter also looks more explicitly to the future. Among the issues discussed are the following. What policy responses are likely to occur as a result of increased competitive pressures? What responses will not occur automatically but should be made if nations seek to promote deeper integration of the world economy? Which of the latter can occur independently from some centralized (across nations) decisionmaking body? Which would require explicit supranational institutions, such as the European Community, and how might these operate? Can one realistically hope to enforce these policies?

As integration begins to encompass countries that differ in their economic development and labor practices by much wider margins than the United States, Canada, and the original six EC nations do—such as Mexico under NAFTA, or the emerging eastern European nations, or the developing economies of Asia, Africa, and Latin America—what special issues arise? For example, should some of the "benefits" from trade that accrue to the more developed countries be directed back to the less developed countries as "transitional subsidies," to allow them to achieve higher standards than their economies can currently afford? If so, how can that be accomplished? Or, how can developed nations guarantee that relatively unskilled workers in their countries are not the big losers from increased economic integration? Will these nations' inability to prevent such losses be a serious obstacle to continued increased economic integration?

Characteristics of Labor Markets

Labor markets and the employment relationship involve much more than the exchange of a worker's labor services for the payment of an hourly or weekly wage. Weekly hours of work are often subject to government, or union-negotiated, rules determining the cost and usage of overtime hours. Annual hours of work are influenced by public and private policies for holidays, vacations, and sick leave, as well as by child care provisions and leave for family reasons. These characteristics of the labor market are discussed in chapter 2.

Various forms of insurance are also provided as part of the employment relationship in most countries. These include unemployment, disability, and retirement income insurance. Although they are often government programs financed by payroll taxes on employees and employers, or by general revenues, in some countries both government and private employers provide retirement income insurance (pensions). Health insurance is currently offered in the United States through a mixed system of private and government provision that leaves many people uncovered. In contrast, coverage in most other developed countries is more universal. The implications of insurance programs for economic integration are discussed in chapter 3.

Either legislatively or through the collective bargaining process, many nations establish labor market standards to assure workers minimally desirable conditions of employment. These include minimum wages, restrictions on the use of child labor, occupational safety and health standards, and standards requiring nondiscrimination by gender, race, ethnicity, age, or disability status. In the debate over NAFTA, labor market standards in Mexico were a primary concern. That issue and others issues related to standards are discussed in chapter 4.

Most nations have policies to facilitate labor market adjustments and to partially compensate workers who become displaced from their jobs. Among these are unemployment insurance, more general income and welfare programs, and training programs. Other policies relate to legally mandated, collectively bargained, or voluntary employer-provided advance notice of potential job loss, severance pay for job loss, and rules that prevent unjust dismissal. Such policies, many of which may be essential if widespread political support for increased economic integration is to occur, are discussed in chapter 5. Also discussed are rules that exempt employers from having to provide coverage for temporary or part-time workers, and the effects of those exemptions.

Two final aspects of labor markets, covered in chapter 6, are the specification of who can work in a country and the rights workers have to determine their work environment. The chapter deals with three main topics: immigration policies and what types of workers, if any, are allowed to migrate into a country; what group—government, professional associations, unions, or a supranational body—decides whether a worker is qualified to work in an occupation; and what system of industrial relations exists in a country, including the rights workers have to be formally involved in discussions over their working conditions.

Unemployment Insurance: An Example

To introduce some of the issues discussed throughout the book, I consider as an example the provision and financing of unemployment insurance (UI) benefits through an employer-based payroll tax. The complexity of the UI system and how it varies across nations (and in the U.S. states) has been discussed by others.[4] Here I initially consider a very simplified program in which the UI tax is specified to be a flat rate of $\$T$ per worker. Initially, I also assume that exchange rates are fixed between nations; an assumption relaxed in the next section.

Consider first a model of the labor market for a nation in the absence of a UI system. The demand for labor is represented by the downward sloping line D_0 and the supply of labor by the upward sloping line S_0 in figure 1-1. If the labor market is competitive, the equilibrium will be at point a, where the wage paid to employees is W_0 and the equilibrium employment level is E_0.

The introduction of a UI system will shift both the demand and the supply curves in this model. On the one hand, because employers must now pay a tax of $\$T$ per worker, the wage they will be willing to pay to employ any given number of workers will decline by exactly the amount of the tax. That is, the demand for labor will shift to D_1, which is everywhere below D_0 by $\$T$.

On the other hand, the provision of UI benefits enhances the attractiveness of entering the labor force, because potential entrants know that if they do enter the labor force and become unemployed at some future

---

4. See, for example, *OECD Employment Outlook, July 1991*, chap. 7; *OECD Employment Outlook, September 1988*, chap. 4; Hamermesh (forthcoming). I revisit UI systems in chapters 3 and 5.

Figure 1-1. *Who Bears the Burden of a Payroll Tax?*

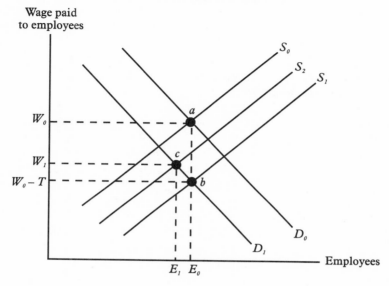

date, they may receive UI benefits during that spell of unemployment. As such, the provision of UI will lead more workers to enter the labor force, and the supply curve will shift to the right.

How much will this supply curve shift? In figure 1-1, I initially *assume* that the benefits workers expect to receive from the tax are just equal to the cost of the tax to employers. If that is so, the supply curve will shift to S_1, and the new labor market equilibrium occurs at point b. There is no change in employment, but the wage paid to workers falls exactly by the amount of the tax. That is, workers fully pay for their UI benefits in the form of lower wages. Since wages have fallen by the amount of the tax, the imposition of the UI tax does not change employers' costs (which now equal the wage rate plus the UI tax) of employing workers, and thus employment remains unchanged.

Suppose, however, that rather than shifting out to S_1, the supply curve shifts only out to S_2 because workers value the benefits at less than their costs to employers. Here the new equilibrium is at point c; wages fall by less the amount of the tax to W_1, and employment falls to E_1. Although workers still bear part of the burden of the tax in the form of lower wages (and employment), employers now also bear part of the burden because their total cost per worker (now $W_1 + T$) is greater than W_0. Insofar as higher labor costs lead employers to increase their product prices, domestic consumers will be worse off. Furthermore, the nation's products will become less competitive on the world market and exports will be reduced. Hence, in a fixed exchange rate world, if a payroll tax to finance UI, or any other social insurance program, is not fully shifted onto workers, it can reduce a nation's international competitive position. Conversely, requiring a potential trading partner to increase the generosity of its UI system, as a precondition to reducing trade barriers, will worsen that nation's competitive position.

Are payroll taxes fully shifted onto workers? Some recent European data suggest that in the long run they may be, although not in the short run. More specifically, the data indicate that a 1 percentage point increase in the payroll tax increases labor costs by about one-half of 1 percentage point in the first year, with nearly half of the labor cost increase still persisting after five years.[5] Furthermore, other studies based on the estimation of wage equations that use data from a number of countries find evidence of only a partial shifting of the tax onto workers even in the long run.[6] Thus the generosity of a nation's UI system, and hence the level of the payroll tax needed to finance it, may well influence trade flows, at least in the short run.[7]

This finding suggests that concern over the generosity of social insurance programs in competitor nations will be part of any movement toward increased economic integration. Indeed, it explains the attempts (not yet successful) by the EC to harmonize labor standards and social insurance programs across member nations.[8] It also explains why some European countries, in the face of increased international competition during the 1980s, tried to reduce the "generosity" of their social programs or the level of their standards in an effort to achieve more "economic flexibility."[9]

UI systems are much more complex than my simple example assumes. Introducing several complications shows other ways in which UI systems may influence, or may be influenced by, increased economic integration.

First, in the United States, UI payroll taxes are assessed on earnings only up to a ceiling level. This "taxable wage base" varies across states but is typically less than $15,000 a year.[10] Consequently, any given percentage point increase in the UI tax rate that is not fully shifted onto workers

5. *OECD Employment Outlook, July 1990,* annex 6A.

6. Hamermesh (1993, table 5.1).

7. In the long run, one would also expect that capital mobility would cause real labor costs per unit of output to equalize across nations and thus that the tax would be fully shifted.

8. See "Social Charter State of Play (1992) for a report on some of their recent efforts.

9. Blank and Freeman (forthcoming).

10. See *Highlights of State Unemployment Compensation Laws, January 1992* (1992, pp. 9–10).

will increase the cost of low-skilled workers relative to the costs of high-skilled workers. Thus UI tax increases may raise the relative cost of goods produced in the United States using unskilled labor and influence the nation's comparative advantage (or disadvantage) in producing goods using unskilled labor.

Second, although some nations finance their regular UI problems out of payroll taxes (like the United States), other countries (like Denmark) finance benefits at least partially out of general revenues. To the extent that the incidence of general revenue and payroll taxes is different, in a fixed exchange rate world the method of financing UI (or other types of social insurance) may influence a nation's competitive position.[11]

Third, in most European countries there is zero experience rating, whereas in the United States there is some, though imperfect, experience rating in the payroll tax.[12] Since imperfect experience rating subsidizes some types of firms (high turnover) at the expense of others (low turn-over), differences in the extent of experience rating across nations will, in theory, affect the types of industries that may find it profitable to relocate across countries.[13]

Fourth, given that an unemployed person is eligible for UI benefits, most nations specify both a minimum benefit level for which a formerly low-wage worker is eligible and a maximum benefit for which a pre-viously high-wage worker is eligible. Differences in these levels may affect the skill classes of workers that migrate in response to earnings dif-ferentials between areas. Migrating to an area with a high minimum (maximum) UI benefit level is likely to be more attractive to relatively low-skilled (high-skilled) individuals. There have been no empirical stud-ies, however, that address, even within the United States (where there are

11. To my knowledge, no empirical study has contrasted the incidence of payroll and nonproportional general revenue (for example, personal and corporate income or value added) taxes. If all taxes are proportional and small, in theory the method of finance should not affect the incidence of the tax.

12. *Experience rating* means that the tax rate a firm pays increases when the workers it employs collect more benefits (either because more workers are laid off or because more are unemployed for a longer time). Experience rating is usually *imperfect* because when more benefits are collected, the tax rate does not increase enough to cover the costs of the additional benefits. The distinction between the United States and Europe may be less important than it appears because, as shown in chapter 5, many European nations require severance pay for employees who are permanently laid off. This creates an implicit form of imperfect experience rating.

13. No one has examined how differences in experience rating in UI tax rates across states influences locational decisions of firms. However, studies of state and local corporate income taxes in the United States typically find that these taxes have little effect on business location across states. For a recent survey of the literature, see Wasylenko (1991).

separate UI systems in each state), whether individuals' migration decisions are sensitive to UI benefit levels.[14]

Finally, rules governing who is eligible for UI may also affect labor mobility. If unemployed workers who are laid off in one jurisdiction immediately become eligible for UI benefits if they move to a new jurisdiction, mobility between jurisdictions will be stimulated. But if people who move across jurisdictions lose their UI benefits, the reverse will be true.

In the United States workers who are eligible to receive UI benefits in one state automatically receive the same level of benefits from a second states's UI fund if they move to that state. Such *interstate claims* are then charged to the first state, which reimburses the second state for its outlays. These interstate claims are not insignificant; they averaged about 4.4 percent of all weeks of UI benefits claimed in the United States in 1989.[15] Consequently, within the United States the system of state UI systems does not interfere with migration; rather it facilitates the migration of unemployed workers from one state to other states that may offer them better employment prospects. The EC currently has a *regulation* that similarly provides for the continuation of UI benefits and thus does not discourage the migration (within the EC) of unemployed workers who are seeking employment in other countries.[16]

Flexible Exchange Rates, Tax Incidence, and Economic Integration

The analysis of the effects of the UI payroll tax just presented implicitly assumed that a system of fixed exchange rates was in place. This

14. However, recent studies in the United States on whether interstate differences in the generosity of welfare benefits influence migration decisions of low-income families do find evidence of an influence. For a review of the evidence, see Moffitt (1992, table 10).

15. U.S. Department of Labor (1991, table 8).

16. Some definitions. EC *regulations* are binding on all member nations. *Directives* are binding as to the results to be achieved, but leave to national governments the decisions on the form and methods to be used to achieve their goals. For example, in the language of occupational safety and health legislation, a standard that mandated the type of safety device that must be installed on a piece of capital equipment would be classified as a regulation; one that required industrial accidents not to exceed a certain level would be classified as a directive. The EC also issues *recommendations* and *opinions,* neither of which are binding. For a discussion of the structure of the EC and how regulations and directives emerge, see the appendix to this chapter.

Regulation 1408/71 deals with the application of social security schemes, including unemployment insurance, to people moving within the EC. Title 3, chapter 6, details the rules governing UI payments. See European Information Services (1990, pp. 635–37).

assumption is probably appropriate for trade between states in the United States and for trade between nations that seek to limit fluctuations in the relative values of their currencies, such as the EC nations. Here I discuss how the introduction of flexible exchange rates alters the analysis.

Consider first the simplified world of figure 1-1, in which an increase in a single flat-rate payroll tax is applied to all employees. To the extent that the tax is not fully shifted onto workers, at least in the short run, their costs, and hence the costs of the nation's products, will rise on the international market. With higher prices, there will be an excess supply of the country's exports, and the country's currency will therefore depreciate relative to its trading partners' currencies. However, the decline in the value of the country's currency will make its trading partners' goods more expensive, and the country will reduce its imports. Thus an increase in the tax will lead to a reduction in trade and a decrease in the nation's standard of living. Put another way, residents of the nation will partially bear the burden of the tax in the form of higher prices for both domestic and foreign goods.

Continuing in this simplified world, suppose now that the nation produces more than one good and that these goods vary in their capital intensity. Since the payroll tax is still being assumed to be a per worker tax, an increase in the tax will cause costs to rise more at low capital-intensive firms than at high capital-intensive firms, as long as the tax is not fully shifted onto workers. Thus the nation's comparative advantage (disadvantage) in producing capital-intensive goods will increase (decrease). Although the resulting depreciation of a nation's currency will lead to a reduction in its imports and a decrease in its standard of living, its exports will shift toward more capital-intensively produced goods.

Finally, suppose that as in the U.S. system, the nation's UI tax is based on payroll, not employment, and that the system has a relatively low maximum taxable wage base. Then an increase in the payroll tax rate that is not fully shifted onto workers will increase the costs of low-skilled workers relative to the costs of high-skilled workers. The nation's comparative advantage (disadvantage) in producing goods that require high-skilled workers will therefore increase (decrease). Although the resulting depreciation of the nation's currency will lead to a reduction in its imports, exports produced using skilled labor will rise relative to those produced using unskilled labor. So employment opportunities for skilled workers will rise relative to employment opportunities for unskilled workers. Put another way, the nation's demand for skilled workers will rise, and its demand for unskilled workers will fall.

Flexible exchange rates, therefore, do *not* alter the basic proposition that increases in payroll taxes which are not fully shifted onto workers will influence trade. In a fixed exchange rate world, the rise in the nation's product price discourages exports. In a flexible exchange rate world, the resulting depreciation of a nation's currency helps to reduce the drop in exports but also leads to a reduction in imports. Hence, under either exchange rate regime, the nation's consumers partially pay for the increase in the payroll tax rate by experiencing higher prices for domestic goods and, under a flexible exchange rate system, by also experiencing higher prices for imports.

Appendix: The European Community and the Labor Market

The European Community was established by the 1957 Treaty of Rome.[17] Originally consisting of six member countries—Belgium, France, West Germany, Italy, Luxembourg, and the Netherlands—that were roughly at the same stage of economic development, its membership was broadened to include Denmark, Ireland, and the United Kingdom in 1973. More recently, three southern European members were admitted: Greece in 1981 and Spain and Portugal in 1986. Several of the latter six nations are at much lower stages of development and have much lower real income levels than the original six member nations have.

The Treaty of Rome had as its goals the raising of living standards and the promotion of improved conditions of employment in member nations. These goals were to be achieved, by reducing barriers to the mobility of goods, capital, and labor. That is, the treaty sought to broaden the scope of European markets and increase their competitiveness.

The Single Europe Act, signed in February 1986, and becoming effective in July 1987, had as its goal the removal of the remaining barriers to a single market by the start of 1993. Unlike the Treaty of Rome, however, the act stressed not only competition but also the goal of establishing minimum standards in the labor market. Harmonization of standards at levels that are higher than those that exist in some member nations is thought to be a way to avoid "social dumping" (the flight of capital to low-cost areas) and thus possible pressure for lower standards. The fear of the United Kingdom that it would lose some of its competitive advantages if the EC took a more activist role in setting labor market policies, and attempts by the EC to begin to move down that road through its 1992 Maastricht Treaty on European Union, led the United

---

17. The appendix draws heavily on Flanagan (1993); Addison and Siebert (1991); Holmstedt (1991, pp. 6–10); Molle (1990, chap. 4).

Kingdom to ratify that treaty only after the nation was allowed to opt out of any future labor market standards that were established.[18]

Governance of the European Community takes place through the EC Commission, the EC Council of Ministers, the European Parliament, and the EC Court of Justice. The focus here is on how EC legislation relating to labor markets is enacted, administered, and enforced by these groups.

The Commission, which consists of seventeen members (two from each of the five largest countries, one from each of the other seven) appointed by EC member states for five-year terms, proposes EC legislation and is the chief administrative body for adopted legislation. The Council, which represents member nations, is responsible for formally adopting legislation. Although historically decisions were made on the basis of unanimity, the Single Europe Act permits "qualified" majority voting on some issues (such as the health and safety of workers). A qualified majority is defined as slightly over 70 percent of the total vote on an issue, with the number of votes each member nation has varying from 10 to 2, according to its size. Council decisions take the form of binding regulations and directives and nonbinding recommendations and opinions.

The European Parliament consists of 518 members, elected directly by residents of member nations, with the number elected by each nation related to its size. The Parliament has no legislative power; it serves primarily as an advisory body that provides opinions on Commission proposals before the Council makes a decision. Under the Single Europe Act, the Council must take the Parliament's views into account on certain issues.

The Court of Justice consists of thirteen judges, five advocate generals, and a registrar. Judges and advocate generals are appointed by the agreement of member states for six-year terms and cannot be dismissed. Alleged violations of EC rules that have not been satisfactorily resolved by the Commission, or through national judicial systems, go to the Court.[19] An advocate general prepares an impartial conclusion based on the evidence; the Court then reviews the conclusion and issues a judgment. The Court relies on member states to enforce its rulings.

18. See "Social Policy and the Maastricht Summit—Confusion Reigns" (1992, pp. 2–3); "Maastricht and Social Policy—Part One" (1993, pp. 14–20).

19. The Commission has the authority to gather information, invite explanations of behavior, request a company or member state to cease a violation, and in some cases impose a fine if the alleged violation continues. Many of the cases that the Court receives deal with whether an existing national law of a member state is in conflict with an EC directive or regulation, not with violations by individual companies.

Chapter 2

Hours of Work and the Statutes That Govern Them

A NNUAL hours of work per employee differ across nations. The principal reasons are variations in public and private policies regarding holidays, vacations, sick leave, and leave for family reasons; variations in the proportion of employees working part time; weekly hours of work often being subject to government or union-negotiated rules governing the usage of overtime hours; and variations in work-leisure preferences.

After presenting data on the variation in hours of work per employee across nations, I examine some of the statutory regulations that may contribute to the variation. I then address whether increased economic integration will necessitate a convergence in these labor market regulations and in annual hours of work.

Hours of Work

Average hours actually worked per employee per year vary widely across nations in the Organization for Economic Cooperation and Development (OECD).[1] In table 2-1, which presents data for selected nations for 1990, annual hours range from 1,417 in Norway to 2,078 in Japan. Considerable variation occurs even among the EC nations. The typical dependent employee in Spain, for example, works about 300 hours more annually than his or her French counterpart.[2]

To some degree, variations in annual hours across nations are due to the variation in the proportion of employees who work part time. Among the nations listed in table 2-1, those with the greatest proportion of

1. The OECD consists of the twelve EC nations, plus Australia, Austria, Canada, Finland, Iceland, Japan, New Zealand, Norway, Sweden, Switzerland, Turkey, and the United States.
2. "Dependent" employment excludes the self-employed and unpaid family workers.

Table 2-1. *Average Hours Worked per Person per Year and Part-Time Employment as a Percent of Total Employment, Selected OECD Nations, 1970, 1979, 1990*[a]

Country	Average annual hours			Part-time employment	
	1970	1979	1990	1979	1990
Total employment					
Canada	1,890	1,794	1,734	12.5	15.4
Finland	1,982	1,859	1,756	6.7	7.2
France (EC)	1,962	1,817	1,678	8.2	12.0
Italy (EC)	1,969	1,788	n.a.	5.3	5.7[b]
Japan	n.a.	2,110	2,078[c]	15.4	17.6[b]
Norway	1,766	1,501	1,417	25.3	26.6
Spain (EC)	n.a.	2,148	1,941	n.a.	4.8
Sweden	1,641	1,451	1,480	23.6	23.2
United States	1,886	1,808	1,782	16.4	16.9
Dependent employment[d]					
France (EC)	1,821	1,667	1,539	8.2	12.0
Germany (EC)	1,885	1,699	1,589	11.4	13.2[b]
Netherlands (EC)	n.a.	1,591	1,433	16.6	33.2
Spain (EC)	n.a.	2,032	1,858	n.a.	4.8
United States	1,836	1,767	1,750	16.4	16.9

Source: *OECD Employment Outlook, July 1992*, p. 280 (average hours); *OECD Employment Outlook, July 1991*, p. 46 (part-time employment).

n.a. Not available.

a. Average annual hours data include part-time workerrs.

b. Data are for 1989.

c. Data are for 1988.

d. Excludes the self-employed and unpaid family workers.

part-time employees in 1990, namely Norway, Sweden, and the Netherlands, also tended to have the shortest average annual hours of work.

The table suggests that over the last thirty years annual hours of work have declined in OECD nations. This decline has occurred for two main reasons. First, it reflects the increase in the proportion of employees working part time, which is partially due to increases in the labor force participation rates of women with children, who often find that part-time employment is more consistent with their family responsibilities than full-time employment.[3] Second, the decline reflects voluntary decisions by full-time workers to reduce their hours of work as their real incomes

3. See the Symposium "Trends in Women's Work, Education and Family Building" (1985).

Table 2-2. *Average Weekly Hours Usually Worked in EC Nations in 1991*

Country	All employees (1)	Full-time employees (2)	Part-time employees (3)	Percent of employees that are part-time (4)	Percent of employees that are female (5)
Belgium	35.6	38.0	20.4	13.3	39.3
Denmark	33.8	38.4	19.2	24.1	48.0
France	37.6	39.7	22.1	12.3	44.5
Germany	36.6	39.8	19.4	15.3	41.3
Greece	39.7	40.3	20.4	2.8	34.7
Ireland	38.5	40.4	18.2	9.0	39.5
Italy	38.0	38.7	25.2	5.1	36.8
Luxembourg	38.4	39.8	21.2	7.5	35.1
Netherlands	31.7	38.9	16.6	32.0	38.2
Portugal	40.9	41.5	21.1	13.2	41.9
Spain	39.6	40.5	18.1	4.2	32.3
United Kingdom	37.3	43.4	17.4	15.4	46.8

Source: *Eurostat Labour Force Survey: Results 1991* [1993, tables 47(A), 55(B), 56(C), 34(D), 25(E)].

increase. That is, they have chosen to consume some of their increased real income in the form of shorter annual hours.

Some of the variation in annual hours of work across nations stems from variations in weekly hours of work. Among the EC nations, weekly hours in 1991 varied from 31.7 in the Netherlands to 40.9 in Portugal (table 2-2, column 1). The range of variation in weekly hours for full-time employees (column 2) was much smaller; hence most of the variation in weekly hours came from the variation in the percentage of employees working part time (column 4).[4] Not surprisingly, as previously noted, this percentage is highly correlated with the percentage of female employees,[5] a figure ranging from about 32 percent in Spain to about 48 percent in Denmark in 1991 (column 5).

Statutes That Influence Hours of Work

Many statutes influence annual hours of work in EC nations. As table 2-3 shows, the number of paid public holidays for which workers

4. The correlation across countries between average weekly hours and the proportion of employees working part time is -.86.
5. The correlation is .54.

Table 2-3. *Statutory Regulation of Holidays, Vacation, and Weekly Hours in EC Nations in 1991*

Country	Public holidays	Annual vacation—paid leave weeks	Maximum weekly hours	Overtime permitted
Belgium	10	4[a]	40	65 hours per 3 months
Denmark	b	5	b	c
France	11	5	39	9 hours a week 130 hours a year + more when authorized
Germany	10–14	3[a]	48	2 hours a day for up to 30 days
Greece	13	4[a]	37.5–40	3 hours a day 18 hours a week 150 hours a year
Ireland	8	3	48–56	2 hours a day 12 hours a week 240 hours a year
Italy	15	b	48	b
Luxembourg	10	5[a]	40	2 hours a day
Netherlands	6[d]	4	48	0.5 to 3.5 hours a day
Portugal	12	3–4	42–44	2 hours a day 160 hours a year
Spain	14	5	40	80 hours a year
United Kingdom	b	b	b	b

Sources: "Daily, Weekly and Yearly Rest and Weekly Hours" (1991); Commission of the European Communities (1992c, tables 4, 6).

a. Service requirement for entitlement.
b. No legislation.
c. Determined by collective bargaining.
d. Plus 1 more every fifth year.

were eligible varied between six and fourteen in 1991 across the ten EC nations that had legislation governing holidays. Similarly, the number of weeks of paid vacation workers were statutorily required to receive ranged between three and five. In most countries workers qualify for such leave after twelve months of service, which gives employers an incentive to try to avoid such costs through the use of short-tenure or temporary workers (an issue discussed in chapter 6).

Weekly hours are statutorily restricted through maximum hours legislation. Several EC countries, such as, Belgium and France, restrict weekly hours to 40 or less. Others, such as Germany and the Netherlands, set a maximum of 48. Still others, such as Denmark and the

Table 2-4. *Sick Leave in EC Nations*

Country	Maximum length of leave	Payment (percent of earnings)
Belgium	52 weeks	60
Denmark	91 weeks in 3 years	90
France	52 weeks in 3 years	50[a]
Germany	78 weeks in 3 years	80
Greece	26 weeks	50
Ireland	52 weeks[b]	Up to 75
Italy	6 months	50[c]
Luxembourg	52 weeks	100
Netherlands	52 weeks	70
Portugal	155 weeks	65[d]
Spain	18 months	60[e]
United Kingdom	28 weeks	52–70

Source: Commission of the European Communities (1992c, table 11).

a. With 3 children 66⅔ percent from 31st day.

b. Unlimited if employee has paid 156 weeks contribution into the system.

c. 66⅔ percent after 21st day.

d. 100 percent if hospitalized and with dependents.

e. From 4th to 20th day; 75 percent thereafter.

United Kingdom, have no maximum weekly hours laws, leaving their determination to collective bargaining. In all EC countries with hours limitations some overtime is permitted, typically with premium pay (table 2-3). Often authorization of governmental units or unions are required for the use of overtime, and collective bargained limitations on hours are often more stringent than those of the statutes.

Nations also differ in the extent to which employees are able to take, and are compensated for, leave for sickness, maternity, or family reasons. Provisions for such leaves are typically part of the social insurance systems in each nation, and the more generous the provisions are the lower one might expect annual hours of work to be. Tables 2–4 and 2–5, respectively, summarize some of these provisions for sickness leave in EC nations and for maternity and parental leave in a broader set of OECD nations.

Durations of maximum sickness leave range from about half a year in some EC countries (Greece, Italy, United Kingdom) to more than a year in others (Denmark, Germany, Portugal). Sick leave payments range from 50 to 100 percent of earnings, and nations that offer more weeks of sick leave also tend to offer higher payments.[6]

6. The correlation is roughly .3.

Table 2-5. *Maternity and Parental Leave Mandated by Government Legislation in 1990, Selected OECD Nations*

| Country | Maternity leave | | Parental leave | | |
| | Maximum duration (weeks) | Replacement rate (percent) | Maximum duration | | Replacement rate (percent) |
			Weeks	Child reaches age	
Australia	52	0	...	...	...
Austria	16	100	...	1 yr.	a
Belgium (EC)	14	100–79.5[b]	...	...	...
Canada	17 or 18[c]	Up to 60	...	...	...
Denmark (EC)	28	90	10	...	a
Finland	17.5	80	28	...	80
France (EC)	16–28[d]	84	...	3 yrs.	a
Germany (EC)	14	100	...	15 mos.	a
Greece (EC)	14	100	...	30 mos.	0
Iceland	13	a	...	...	...
Ireland (EC)	14	60	...	...	...
Italy (EC)	20	80	...	3 yrs.	0
Japan	14	60	...	...	...
Luxembourg (EC)	16	100	...	...	...
Netherlands (EC)	16	100	...	...	...
New Zealand	14	0	...	1 yr.	0
Norway	26–35[e]	100 or 80[e]	52	...	f
Portugal (EC)	13	100	...	3 yrs.	a
Spain (EC)	16	75	156	...	0
Sweden	12	90	...	1 yr.	90[g]
United Kingdom (EC)	18	90[h]	...	...	...
United States	13	0	13	...	0

Sources: Author's interpretation of material in *OECD Employment Outlook, July 1990*, table 5.8, and *Family Medical Leave Act of 1993* (1993).

a. Fixed allowance.
b. Declines with duration of leave.
c. Varies by province.
d. Increases with number of children.
e. 100 percent if 26 weeks are taken; 80 percent if 35 are taken.
f. Sliding scale.
g. 90 percent for the first six weeks; fixed allowance thereafter.
h. As of 1993.

Maternity and parental leave provisions vary widely across nations. As seen in table 2-5, virtually all OECD nations provide for maternity leave; these provisions vary from twelve to fifty-two weeks. Whereas all the EC nations provide for paid maternity leave, with payments coming from each nation's social insurance system, other OECD nations—for example, Australia, New Zealand, and the United States—provide for only unpaid maternity leave.

Statutory parental leave provisions are less prevalent. When they exist, their maximum duration is specified either in terms of weeks or in terms of the age of children. In the latter case, families typically receive a specified allowance per child so that the parent can remain at home while the child is young. In the former case, parental leave is normally intended more for shorter emergency situations. In 1990 fewer than half of the EC nations had statutes providing for paid parental leave.

Likelihood of the Convergence of Hours of Work and the Statutes Governing Them

Do the statutes that govern weekly and annual hours of work in each nation actually influence hours of work? Or do they instead simply reflect underlying economic forces and the preferences of employers and employees? It is interesting that in the United States average weekly hours of work in manufacturing fell from 51.0 in 1909 to 44.2 in 1929. This major decline in weekly hours occurred before the 1938 passage of the Fair Labor Standards Act, which established a time-and-a-half premium for weekly hours worked in excess of 42 in 1938 and in excess of 40 thereafter.[7] In the fifty-five years since the passage of the act, the decline in average weekly hours of work in manufacturing has been much smaller.[8] Hence, for the United States at least, one can argue that hours of work legislation followed a change in underlying economic forces rather than caused them.

Do weekly hours statutes even matter? To a large extent this depends on whether employers and employees comply with them. Evidence from U.S. data suggests that 10 to 25 percent of the people working overtime who, under the law, should be receiving a premium of time and a half fail to receive *any* overtime premium at all.[9]

To my knowledge similar studies do not exist for other countries, but evidence suggests that noncompliance may occur in some EC nations as well. Table 2-6 presents data for every EC nation from the 1991 *Eurostat Labour Force Survey* on the percentage of full-time employees who usually worked 46 or more hours a week. The underlying survey question-

7. Ehrenberg and Schumann (1982, p. 3).

8. In 1992 average weekly hours in manufacturing in the United States were 41.0, and they never fell below 38.9 during the preceding thirty years. See U.S. Department of Labor (1993, p. 82).

9. Ehrenberg and Schumann (1982); Trejo (1991).

Table 2-6. *Percent of Full-Time Employees Who Usually Worked Forty-six or More Hours per Week in 1991, EC Nations*

Country	Percent	Country	Percent	Country	Percent
Belgium	3.0	Spain	6.7	Luxembourg	4.1
Denmark	6.0	France	7.3	Netherlands	2.3
Germany	6.7	Ireland	11.6	Portugal	8.1
Greece	14.1	Italy	8.5	United Kingdom	27.8

Source: *Eurostat Labour Force Surveys: Results 1991* (1993, table 49).

naires made it clear that people were being asked their weekly hours on their *primary* job, not their hours on all jobs.[10] Thus these percentages reflect individuals' weekly hours of work on their full-time jobs.

Consider three examples. Maximum weekly hours were set at 40 in Belgium in 1991, and 65 hours per overtime per three-month period were permitted (table 2–3). That is equivalent to a maximum permitted workweek, including overtime, of 45 hours. Yet, as the data in table 2-6 show, 3 percent of Belgium employees usually worked at least 46 hours a week. Similarly, maximum weekly hours were set at 40 in Spain, with only 80 hours a year of overtime permitted. Yet 6.7 percent of Spanish employees usually worked 46 hours or more, and indeed 9.1 percent usually worked 43 hours or more.[11] People who usually work 43 hours or more work more than 80 hours of overtime a year. Finally, as table 2-6 indicates, maximum weekly hours were statutorily set at 40 in Greece in 1991, and no more than 150 hours of overtime a year were permitted. Clearly Greece's maximum permissible usual workweek, including overtime hours, was less than 45 hours. Yet, as seen in the table, 14.1 percent of Greek full-time employees usually worked at least 46 hours a week in 1991.

These data do not permit us to ascertain if required overtime premium payments were always made to workers from EC nations who worked overtime, another way in which noncompliance may take place. But they do suggest that noncompliance with maximum hours legislation does occur in the EC nations as well as in the United States.

Why should weekly hours of work for full-time workers (table 2-2) be as high in many EC nations as they are? In a number of these nations unions have pushed for shorter work weeks for many years as a way to increase leisure time for employed workers and to spread the available work. Why have employers resisted such changes, given the double-digit

10. *Eurostat Labour Force Sample Survey: Methods and Definitions* (1985, pp. 21–44).
11. *Eurostat Labour Force Survey: Results 1991* (1993, table 49).

rates of unemployment that persisted in many EC nations in the early 1990s? In part the answer is that the extensive vacation and holiday pay required by statute in many EC nations gives employers an incentive to expand hours of work (or at least avoid contracting them) rather than to expand employment. An employer who hires a new employee must provide holiday and vacation pay for him or her, whereas no such costs are incurred if the existing work force is employed longer hours.[12]

Will nations need to harmonize their provisions regarding sick leave, maternity leave, personal leave, and holiday and vacation leave to facilitate economic integration and to avoid "social dumping," or the movement of jobs to countries with low benefit levels? Some people argue yes. However, in most EC nations sick leave, maternity leave, and family leave are financed by payroll taxes on employers and employees, and as noted in chapter 1, the burden of these taxes appears to fall primarily, though not entirely, on employees. That is, the increased worker protection that these types of leave appear to buy is at least partially paid for by workers in the form of lower wages. On balance, then, mandating more generous programs in nations that currently have less generous programs will lead to some, but not a proportionate, increase in labor costs in those nations.

The evidence on mandated benefits provided directly by employers, such as holiday and vacation pay, is less clear. No econometric study conclusively demonstrates that the costs of more generous holiday and vacation leaves are shifted onto workers in the form of lower wages. One U.S. study, however, shows that the costs of state-mandated benefits for maternity leaves are substantially shifted onto workers in the form of lower wages.[13] Another study shows that employers' total compensation costs (wages, benefits, and payroll taxes) for homogeneous types of highly skilled employees tend to equalize across twelve OECD nations.[14] This second study implies that such employees do pay for more generous mandated or negotiated benefits in the form of lower wages. Similarly, cruder aggregate evidence is available which shows that, across nations,

12. Ehrenberg and Schumann (1982); Hart (1988); Hart (1987). In late 1993 the French government proposed cutting the standard workweek by 15 percent, cutting weekly pay 5 percent, and reducing the payroll taxes used to finance unemployment insurance and welfare payments by 5 percent. The government hoped that if labor could increase its productivity by 5 percent, employers could increase employment by 15 percent, thereby reducing unemployment and the government's need for payroll tax revenue. See Peter Passell, "A Four-Day Workweek Plan Is Optimistic, Not Realistic," *New York Times,* November 25, 1993, p. D2. This proposal ignored, however, the large incentive employers have to expand weekly hours to reduce the number of employees to whom they must make holiday and vacation payments.

13. Gruber (1992a); Gruber (1992b).

14. Abowd and Bognanno (forthcoming). The authors study the compensation of chief executive officers, top human resource directors, and manufacturing operatives.

output per employee is much more highly correlated with total employer cost per employee than it is with wage cost per employee.[15] This evidence again suggests that workers pay for at least a good share of their benefits in the form of lower wages.

Insofar as this evidence is correct, to require a country to improve its leave policies as a precondition for increased economic integration is unlikely to greatly affect total labor cost per output in the country. Put another way, unless all elements of the compensation package, including wages, are subject to minimum standards, when such standards are imposed employers can adjust other elements of the compensation package to keep their total costs from rising very much.[16] Attempts to harmonize standards will thus not totally prevent social dumping unless wage levels are included in the standards. Except for minimum wages (see chapter 4), no one has seriously argued that wage levels in a nation should be part of the negotiations over increased economic integration. Hence harmonization of leave policies will probably not be a precondition for increased economic integration.

Will increased economic integration require, or cause, increased convergence in hours of work? Here again the answer is probably no. To the extent that individuals' preferences for income and leisure differ across nations, so will their hours of work. Increased competitive pressure will put pressure on employers to choose levels of hours that will maximize their profits. But if benefit structures and wage levels continue to vary across nations, so too, from employers' perspectives, will optimal hours.

15. This assertion is made by Mitchell and Rojot (1993). Statistical analyses to support it are found in appendix table A3 of the March 1991 draft of their chapter, which is available from Mitchell at the Anderson School of Management at the University of California, Los Angeles.

16. An exception is for workers earning the country's minimum wage. Since the costs of increases in benefits for these workers cannot be shifted onto them in the form of lower wages, more generous leave policies will necessarily increase employers' costs for these workers and will led to a reduction in their employment levels.

Chapter 3

Social and Private Insurance

V IRTUALLY all developed nations, and many developing nations, operate one or more social insurance programs.[1] Although the specific
programs vary across countries, they include (1) *sickness, maternity, and
invalidity* programs that provide replacement of earnings for short-term
illnesses, maternity and family leave benefits, medical benefits (health
insurance), and replacement of earnings for nonwork-related injuries or
illnesses; (2) *old-age and survivors* programs that provide retirement benefits for the aged and benefits for dependent survivors; (3) *employment
injury and occupational disease* programs that cover medical costs and
earnings replacement for work-related injuries and occupational illnesses; (4) *unemployment* programs that provide replacement of earnings
for unemployed workers; and (5) *family allowance* programs that provide
cash benefits for dependents, often with an age limit test.

While these programs are usually (but not always) financed by government, the services provided may come from the private sector. So, for
example, while medical care is primarily a governmental service in the
United Kingdom through its national health insurance system, in Germany a competitive system of private health providers exists. Moreover,
in some countries private financing and provision of certain types of
insurance coexist with, or substitute for, public financing and provision.
In the United States, for instance, a private pension system coexists with
the social security retirement system, and currently health insurance,
except for the elderly (medicare) and poor (medicaid), is a privately
financed and operated system.

Table 3-1 illustrates how three major social insurance programs—retirement, sickness, and unemployment—are financed in each of the EC

1. U.S. Department of Health and Human Services (1992).

24

Table 3-1. *Financing of Social Insurance Programs in EC Nations, July 1, 1988*[a]

Country	Old age and survivor	Sickness, maternity, and invalidism	Unemployment
Belgium	E, W	E, W	E, W
Denmark	E, W, T	T	E, W
France	E(c), W(c)	E, W	E(c), W(c)
Germany	E(c), W(c)	E(c), W(c)	E(c), W(c)
Greece	E(c), W(c)	E(c), W(c)	E(c), W(c)
Ireland	E(c), W(c)	E(c), W(c)	E(c), W(c)
Italy	E, W	E, W	E
Luxembourg	E(c), W(c)	E(c), W(c)	T
Netherlands	W(c)	E(c), W(c)	E(c), W(c)
Portugal	E, W	E, W	E, W
Spain	E(c), W(c)	E(c), W(c)	E(c), W(c)
United Kingdom	E, W(c)	E, W(c)	E, W(c)

Source: Author's interpretation of material in *Comparative Tables of the Social Security Schemes in the Member States of the European Communities* (1989, table II-1).

a. E is employer payroll tax; W is employee payroll tax; (c) is ceiling on payroll tax; T is general tax revenue.

nations. Payroll taxes, often paid by both employers and employees, are the primary means of financing each. In some countries employers or employees do not have to pay any further payroll taxes once an employee's earnings exceed a ceiling level (referred to as the taxable wage base in the United States). Some countries also finance part or all of their programs out of general revenues. Medical benefits in Denmark and unemployment insurance benefits in Luxembourg, for example, are totally financed out of general revenues.

The costs to employers of public and private insurance programs vary widely across nations. Table 3-2 shows these costs as a percentage of hourly compensation for manufacturing production workers in twenty-five countries in 1989. The figures range from 3.2 percent in Hong Kong to almost 32 percent in France. Even within the EC nations, they range from 6 percent in Denmark (where some retirement and all medical benefits are financed from general revenues), to 15 percent in the United Kingdom, to over 30 percent in France and Italy. The wide variation in employer costs across nations does not necessarily imply that nations with high insurance and benefits costs place themselves at serious competitive disadvantages in the international economy. For, as discussed in chapter 1, empirical evidence suggests that at least some of these costs are shifted onto employees in the form of lower wages.

Table 3-2. *Social Insurance Expenditures and Other Labor Taxes as a Percent of Hourly Compensation Costs of Production Workers in Manufacturing, Selected Countries, 1989* [a]

Country	Percent	Country	Percent
France (EC)	31.8	Korea	17.0
Italy (EC)	31.7	Switzerland	16.0
Sweden	30.3	Australia	15.2
Spain (EC)	28.6[b]	Luxembourg (EC)	15.2[c]
Austria	27.8	United Kingdom (EC)	15.1
Belgium (EC)	26.2	Ireland (EC)	14.8
Netherlands (EC)	23.1	Japan	13.1
Finland	22.6	Singapore	12.2
Germany (EC)	21.9	Canada	11.6
Portugal (EC)	22.1	Denmark (EC)	6.0
Norway	22.0	Taiwan	4.8
United States	19.7	Hong Kong	3.2
Greece (EC)	18.1[b]		

Source: U.S. Department of Labor (1990a, table 13).

a. Included in social insurance expenditures and other labor taxes are employer expenditures for legally required insurance programs and contractual and private benefit plans (for example, health insurance in the United States).

b. Data are for 1988.

c. Data are for 1987.

This chapter focuses on two aspects of social insurance systems, retirement and medical insurance, and their likely impact on, and interaction with, increased economic integration.

Retirement Systems

Most EC nations finance their public retirement systems by a payroll tax on employers and employees (table 3-1). In the Netherlands the tax is nominally levied only on workers, and in Denmark a portion of the system is also financed by general revenue.

Six EC nations have annual earnings ceilings after which no further employer contributions are required. Table 3-3 presents the level of these ceilings in 1988 (column 1), average hourly earnings in manufacturing in the country that year (column 2), and then using data on annual hours worked per person in the country (column 3), contrasts the ceiling level to annual earnings in manufacturing (column 4). The ceilings range from roughly 1.8 to 2.5 times average annual earnings. Hence only for relatively high-wage workers do additional hours of work, at the margin, *not*

Table 3-3. *Annual Earnings Ceilings after Which No Additional Employer Payroll Tax Payments for Old-Age and Survivors Benefits Were Required, Selected EC Nations, 1988*

Country	Ceiling (1)	Hourly earnings in manufacturing (2)	Annual hours worked per person per year (3)	Ceiling/average annual earnings in manufacturing (4)
France	Fr 121,320	41.79	1,546	1.880
Germany	DM 72,000	18.33	1,623	2.421
Greece	Dr 169,825[a]	459.70	n.a.	2,463[b]
Ireland	Punt 16,200	4.90	n.a.	1.838[b]
Luxembourg	Flux 1,324,464	357.00	n.a.	2.062[b]
Spain	PTA 267,780[a]	735.00	1,843	2.375

Sources: Numbers in columns 1–3 are author's calculations from data in, respectively, *Comparative Tables of the Social Security Schemes in the Member States of the European Communities* (1989, table II-1); International Labour Office (1992, table 17A); *OECD Employment Outlook, July 1991*, table L. Numbers in column 4 are author's calculations.

n.a. Not available.

a. Per month.

b. Assumed value of 1,800 hours used in the calculations.

require payment of the tax. So only for these high-paid employees does the tax create an incentive for employers to expand hours rather than employment (see chapter 2).

Not surprisingly, different tax rates across nations lead to different benefit levels. The top half of table 3-4 shows the gross retirement income replacement rates in six EC nations for workers permanently attached to the labor force who are at different levels of earnings and different marital status. A single worker earning the average manufacturing wage would face a gross replacement rate of 77 percent in Portugal but only 33 percent in the Netherlands. The range in gross replacement rates is even wider for high-wage workers; however, since high-wage workers usually have the highest probability of also being covered by a private pension plan, the actual range may not be as wide as it looks.[2]

Since the tax treatment of earned and retirement income is different in many countries, the bottom half of table 3-4 presents net income replacement ratios. Again the differences are wide, varying for the typical single worker from about 50 percent in the Netherlands to almost 95 percent in Portugal.

How can differences in replacement rates, and hence employers' payroll taxes, persist across the EC nations? As discussed in chapter 1,

2. Gustman, Mitchell, and Steinmeier (1993).

Table 3-4. *Income Replacement Rates in Compulsory Pension Plans in Six EC Nations, 1991*
Percent

Country	Wage relative to average in manufacturing					
	Without spouse			With spouse		
	⅔	1	2	⅔	1	2
	Gross income replacement rate					
Belgium	59	47	36	73	58	43
Denmark	53	53	39	53	53	39
France	78	69	59	78	69	59
Luxembourg	76	67	54	76	67	54
Netherlands	50	33	17	72	48	24
Portugal	77	77	77	84	82	79
	Net income replacement rate					
Belgium	81	73	53	91	80	62
Denmark	72	77	63	66	69	55
France	96	88	75	94	83	73
Luxembourg	86	78	69	85	77	65
Netherlands	66	49	27	90	67	37
Portugal	89	94	102	95	98	103

Source: *Eurostat Rapid Reports: Population and Social Conditions 1991.6* (1991, tables 1, 2).

at least some of the difference in employers' costs, and hence employees' benefits, appears to be shifted back onto workers in the form of lower wages. To some extent then, more generous public retirement systems seem merely to alter the form in which compensation is received, rather than alter employers' total costs. That is, they do not change a nation's international competitiveness by as much as crude comparisons of differences in public pension costs might suggest.

Do public retirement systems currently encourage or discourage increased economic integration? In the United States the federal social security system covers workers in all states, and retirement benefits are based on career earnings in all covered employment. Thus this single national system facilitates movement of workers across employers and geographic areas (states). Many state governments have their own public retirement systems for state and local government employees. An individual's retirement benefits under these systems is usually determined by his or her average earnings and years of service while a public employee in the state. Often these plans allow an employee to receive service credit for years worked in other states by permitting the employee to

Table 3-5. *Minimum Period of Membership Required to Receive Retirement Benefits under EC Nations' Social Security Programs, 1988*

Country	Period	Country	Period
Belgium	None	Ireland	156 contribution weeks and average at least 24 weeks a year
Denmark	3 years of residence	Italy	15 years of contributions
France	None	Luxembourg	120 months of insurance
Germany	60 months of insurance	Netherlands	None
Greece	4,050 working days	Portugal	120 months of contributions
Spain	At least 10 years	United Kingdom	52 weeks plus coverage in at least 9/40 of years of potential work life

Sources: *Comparative Tables of the Social Security Schemes of the Member States of the European Communities* (1989), table VII-1; (for the United Kingdom) U.S. Department of Health and Human Services (1992).

make payments to "buy" into the system for these years.[3] Such schemes obviously facilitate the mobility of public employees across states.

There is no single multinational social security system in the EC; however, EC regulations 1408/71 and 574/72 attempt to facilitate economic integration by requiring that migrants be covered by the social security system in the country in which they work on the same basis as natives are covered.[4] If a person works during her lifetime in more than one country, she would accrue retirement benefits from both countries based on her work experience in each. So, for example, if she worked ten years in one country and twenty years in a second, and thirty years were required in each for a "normal" retirement benefit, she would receive one-third of a normal pension from the first country and two-thirds of a normal pension from the second.

Although this regulation facilitates intercountry mobility of labor to its most productive use, and hence economic integration, most of the EC nations' retirement systems have minimum membership requirements that must be satisfied before a person can receive benefits under the systems. For example, in Denmark three years of residence are required, in Germany sixty months of work are required, and in Italy fifteen years of work are required (table 3-5). Such minimum residence or service requirements, other things equal, discourage mobility of labor across countries when prospective employment opportunities in other countries are thought to be only temporary.

3. For a description of these provisions for New York State teachers, see, for example, *Compilation of Laws Covering New York State Teachers' Retirement System, As Amended through August 15, 1992* (1992, pp. 24–27).

4. European Information Services (1990, pp. 580–945).

Mindful of this fact, EC regulation 1408/71 provides that when the years an immigrant worked in a foreign country do meet the minimum membership requirement under the country's system, they may be credited to the immigrant's home country's system in computing the retirement benefits she will be eligible for in her home country.[5] Thus this provision of the regulation facilitates even the temporary mobility of labor to its most productive uses.

The EC experience suggests that explicit harmonization of retirement benefits, either in level or replacement rate form, is not required to facilitate economic integration. Indeed, if increased benefits were fully passed on to workers in the form of lower wages, harmonization of benefits would have no effect on employers' total labor costs and their international competitiveness. But insofar as only part of the costs of increased benefits are shifted onto workers, as chapter 1 suggests, increased benefit levels *will* reduce a nation's potential gains from trade unless the higher benefits lead to increased productivity.[6]

Private pension systems will also likely be influenced by, and influence, the extent of economic integration. In the United States, for example, private pension plans are typically either of the *defined contribution* or *defined benefit* type. Under defined contribution plans, the employer makes a contribution each year for each employee to an annuity fund; this contribution is often specified as a fixed percentage of the employee's earnings. Each year an individual's "fund" grows by the amount of the new contribution and by the tax-free investment return on the fund's existing assets. Upon retirement, the individual receives a retirement annuity based on his age and the value of his fund's assets. The pension benefits a worker receives from a defined contribution plan obviously depend on the plan's investment return.

Defined contribution pension plans can be completely portable. One example of such a plan is the TIAA-CREF system, which covers faculty at most universities in the United States.[7] Each participating university makes contributions into the fund for each of its employees each year; however, the assets in an individual's account "stay with him" if he moves to another institution. The TIAA-CREF system thus encourages mobility of faculty across academic institutions. By analogy, a multinational private defined contribution pension system

5. Holmstedt (1990, p. 105).

6. To the extent that compensation profiles (including pensions) are structured to encourage long-term attachment of workers and firms, they may enhance productivity through inducing increased specific training and work effort. See Gustman, Mitchell, and Steinmeier (1993, pp. 19–29).

7. For a description, see Teachers Insurance and Annuity Association, College Retirement and Equity Fund (TIAA-CREF), *Annual Report*, various years.

would facilitate mobility of workers across countries and thus economic integration.

Defined benefit pension plans do not specify the contribution that an employer must make, but rather the benefit provided to the employee upon retirement. Even though the benefit formula are usually complicated and often include provisions for vesting, death benefits, spousal survival benefits, early retirement options, cost-of-living increases, and implicit penalties for failing to retire by a "normal" retirement age, a typical simplified benefit formula for an individual retiring at the normal retirement age can be expressed as[8]

$$(3\text{-}1) \qquad\qquad\qquad B = ksy.$$

Here B represents the individual's annual pension benefits, k is a measure of the generosity of the plan, s is the individual's years of service with the employer and, y is a measure of his average annual career earnings. So, for example, if k was 0.02 and s was thirty years, the individual would receive 0.60 of his average annual career earnings each year in the form of pension income.

If k was the same across employers, all employers paid the same wages, and y was the individual's average annual earnings during his career, an individual's changing employers during his work life would not reduce his total pension income.[9] However, if y is based on a measure of the individual's earnings during his peak earning year, or highest three earnings years with an employer, mobility would reduce his total pension earnings.[10] Because many defined pension plans are of this form, one must conclude that defined benefit pension plans reduce worker mobility and thus will restrict the flow of labor to its most productive use. So to the extent that greater economic integration increases the desirability of worker mobility, one might expect to see a shift from defined benefit toward defined contribution pension plans.[11]

8. See Barnow and Ehrenberg (1979).

9. To understand this, consider a simple model in which an individual works for two periods, has two equivalent employers, (regardless of which employer he works for he will earn $20,000 in the first and $40,000 in the second period), and has an annual retirement income from each employer of 0.25 (periods worked for the employer × average earnings while at the employer). If the employee spends his career with one employer, his annual retirement income is given by 0.25 (2) ($30,000), or $15,000. If he works one period for each employer, his annual retirement income is 0.25 ($20,000) + 0.25 ($40,000), which again equals $15,000.

10. Consider the example in note 9, but now suppose that the pension formula is based on the highest salary an individual earned with an employer. If the worker spends both periods with one employer, his annual pension income is 0.25 (2) ($40,000), or $20,000. If he works one period for each, his pension income is 0.25 ($20,000) + 0.25 ($40,000), or $15,000, some 25 percent lower.

11. For evidence that this shift is occurring, see Beller and Lawrence (1992).

Such a shift and the accompanying increased mobility of employees, will not necessarily lead to greater economic efficiency for two reasons. First, increased employee turnover reduces employers' incentives to provide firm-specific training, and lower levels of training lead to lower levels of productivity.[12] Second, increased employee mobility limits employers' ability to strategically use the shape of life-cycle compensation profiles to stimulate all employees to exert more effort.[13] These efficiency losses must be weighted against the efficiency gains expected from increased economic integration.

One last aspect of retirement systems warrants mention. Before 1978 many private and public employers in the United States had provisions in their retirement systems requiring employees to retire by a specified age.[14] The passage of the 1978 and 1986 amendments to the Age Discrimination in Employment Act effectively prohibited such mandatory retirement requirements for most American workers. Other nations, however, still permit mandatory retirement rules. For example, although many large employers "guarantee" employees life-time employment, over 97 percent of all Japanese employers currently require their employees to retire by age sixty.[15]

Mandatory retirement rules have been rationalized by some economists as an important component of lifetime compensation schemes that induces employees to increase their productivity and thus benefit *both* employers and employees.[16] Others, however, may view such rules as a way of replacing older, highly paid workers by cheaper younger workers. Insofar as the latter view is widely held, nations that permit mandatory retirement could be accused of allowing employers to discriminate against their older workers and of reaping an unfair cost advantage vis-à-vis nations that do not permit mandatory retirement.

As discussed in chapter 4, some individuals and organizations argue that increased economic integration with a foreign nation should take place *only if* workers' rights are guaranteed in that nation. One might think that these individuals and organizations would be in favor of requiring, as a precondition for increased economic integration, that foreign nations outlaw mandatory retirement as the United States has done. To my knowledge, however, no proponents of protecting workers' rights has made such an argument. Whether this reflects their belief that, contrary to its prohibition in American law, mandatory retirement may

12. Becker (1975).
13. Lazear (1979).
14. Lazear (1979).
15. Rebick (1993, p. 103).
16. Lazear (1979).

Table 3-6. *Health Expenditures and Health Outcomes in EC Nations and the United States*

Country	Health expenditures as a percent of GDP, 1987 (1)	Health expenditures per capita as percent of U.S. per capita expenditures, 1987 (2)	Life expectancy at birth, 1988 (3)	Infant mortality rate, 1988[a] (4)
Belgium	7.2	43	75.4	8
Denmark	6.0	39	75.3	7
France	8.6	54	75.7	9
Germany	8.2	53	75.8	8
Greece	5.3	16	77.0	12
Ireland	7.4	27	n.a.	n.a.
Italy	6.9	41	76.7	8
Luxembourg	7.5	51	n.a.	n.a.
Netherlands	8.5	51	77.1	8
Portugal	6.4	19	74.1	16
Spain	6.0	25	77.1	11
United Kingdom	6.1	37	75.1	9
United States	11.2	100	75.3	11

Source: Mitchell and Rojot (1993, p. 146).

n.a. Not avaialble.

a. Number of deaths per 1,000 children aged less than one year.

be beneficial to workers as a group, or is simply an oversight on their part, is unclear. What is clear more generally, however, is that there may be no universal agreement on whether the existence of a standard or law actually "protects workers' rights."

Medical Care

Table 3-6 presents data for 1987 on aggregate health care expenditures in the United States and the EC nations. Expenditures are expressed both as a percent of GDP (column 1) and on a per capita basis relative to the U.S. per capita expenditure level (column 2). Health care expenditures vary across nations for many reasons, including differences in the age distribution of populations and differences in real income levels; however, clearly the United States spends much more on health care than its EC counterparts do. Indeed, on a per capita basis, the United States spent almost twice as much as any EC nation in 1987 (column 2).

Measuring the outcomes of health care expenditures is not a trivial task. For example, it is difficult to quantify such things as the value of having the freedom to choose one's own doctors, to see them promptly, and to be able to go to medical specialists without prior approval of a "gatekeeper" general practitioner. Even so, two outcomes are often focused on: individuals' life expectancies at birth and infant mortality rates. These outcomes are listed in columns 3 and 4 of the table.

It should be clear from the table that higher health expenditures per se do not guarantee better health outcomes. Indeed, there is virtually no connection between a nation's relative per capita health care expenditure level and its citizens' average life expectancy, and only weak evidence that higher levels of the former are associated with lower infant mortality rates.[17] Although factors other than medical expenditures influence these health outcomes—for example, infant mortality rates depend on family income, and life expectancies depend on dietary and cigarette smoking patterns—these crude comparisons suggest that increased health expenditures do not necessarily improve health status.

Suppose that two otherwise identical nations each finances its health care expenditures through employers, either by an explicit payroll tax that funds a government system or through employer-based purchase of private health insurance for employees. Suppose that the cost of health insurance per worker is twice as much in the second nation as it is in the first but that health outcomes in the two nations are the same. One can interpret this case as showing that the second nation's health care system is less efficient (that is, same health outcomes but higher cost). In the context of the simple supply and demand model presented in figure 1-1, this is a situation in which, relative to an initial equilibrium in which no health insurance is provided, the demand curve for labor would shift down by twice as much in the second country as in the first. However, the supply curve would shift out by the same amount in both countries, since workers in both countries effectively obtain the same health care benefits.

That situation is illustrated in figure 3-1. Here D_0 and S_0 are the assumed identical demand and supply curves for labor in the two countries in the absence of health insurance, D_1 and D_2 are the demand curves with insurance, which is assumed to cost T and $2T$, respectively, and S_3 is the assumed identical supply curve in both countries in the presence of health insurance.

17. The correlation between relative per capita health care expenditures and life expectancy is −.13 if the United States is included and .04 if it is excluded from the analysis. The correlations between relative expenditures and infant mortality rates are −.31 and −.29 in the two cases.

Figure 3-1. *Increases in a Nation's Labor Cost Due to Inefficient Provision of Medical Care*

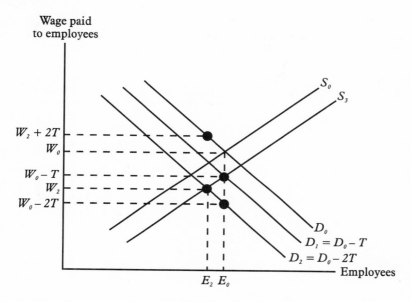

Initially, in the absence of health insurance, the wage in both countries is W_0 and the employment level is E_0. For simplicity, suppose that the cost of health insurance in the efficient health care producing nation (nation 1) is fully shifted onto workers; that is, that the wage in nation 1 falls to $W_0 - T$. Nation 1's employment level remains at E_0, and its employers' costs per worker (wages plus health benefits) remain at W_0.

Note, however, that with a supply curve of S_3, nation 2's wage will fall to W_2 and its employment level to E_2. W_2 is greater than $W_0 - 2T$, and so nation 2's employers' costs per worker (wages + health insurance) of $W_2 + 2T$ are greater than W_0. Hence the cost of health insurance has *not* been fully shifted onto workers in the inefficient health care providing nation, and nation 2's employers have been placed at a competitive disadvantage in the international market.

This example highlights that both the generosity of a health care system, in terms of its costs, and the efficiency of the system, in terms of the benefits it provides, influence a nation's labor costs. Increased economic integration places greater competitive pressure on employers and thus may lead to pressure for reforms that improve the efficiency of the health care systems. Although that is not the only reason, nor even necessarily the main reason, for the pressures for health care

Table 3-7. *Health Care Coverage under EC Nations' Social Security Systems, 1988*

Country	Coverage	Qualifying period
Belgium	Employees, pensioners, unemployed, disabled, students, dependents	6 months
Denmark	All residents	6 weeks
France	Employees, pensioners, unemployed, dependents	1,200 hours work a year, or 600 hours in 6 months, or 200 hours in 3 months
Germany	Employees, pensioners, unemployed, students and those in training, disabled, dependents	None
Greece	Employees, pensioners, unemployed, dependents	50 days of work in preceding year
Ireland	Full eligibility at low-income threshold; limited eligibility for rest of population; dependents	None
Italy	All residents (including foreigners)	None
Luxembourg	Employees, pensioners, unemployed, dependents	None
Netherlands	Employees, pensioners, unemployed, dependents	None
Portugal	All insured and their dependents	None
Spain	Employees, pensioners, unemployed, dependents	None
United Kingdom	All residents	None

Source: *Comparative Tables of the Social Security Schemes* (1989, tables III-1, III-2).

reform that arose in the United States in the early 1990s (see below), it certainly was a contributing factor.

Coverage under the health care systems of all the EC nations are virtually universal. Several nations—namely, Belgium, Denmark, Greece, and France—have a minimum residency or employment requirement that a new migrant to the country must satisfy before he or she is eligible for health care coverage (table 3-7). Although such provisions, in themselves, discourage mobility of labor, title 3 of EC regulation 1408/71 explicitly grants residents of member states "credit" for prior residency or employment in their home countries.[18] Thus the health care coverage

18. European Information Services (1990, p. 599).

systems in the EC do not limit the mobility of workers across national boundaries.

In contrast, in the United States health insurance for all but the aged (medicare) and poor (medicaid) is primarily provided by employers. Increasingly, to reduce their health insurance costs, many employers completely or partially deny coverage to new employees, or their dependents, who have preexisting medical problems. A growing body of research suggests that such provisions excluding preexisting conditions discourage people with preexisting conditions from changing employers.[19] That is, preexisting exclusion provisions create a form of job lock.

Increasing international economic integration manifests itself in greater competitive pressure on employers, and that leads to less job security for workers. Individuals who are forced to change their jobs involuntarily may find themselves without health insurance if they, or a family member, have a preexisting condition. That, in turn, has increasingly led to pressure to reform the American health care system and move it toward universal coverage. This is a second route by which increased economic integration has led to pressure for changes in the American health care system.

Because the American health care system tends to be employment based, it does provide an additional incentive for unemployed workers to try to find employment quickly.[20] Table 3-8 presents information for 1989 on long-term unemployment as a percent of total unemployment for adult men and women in the United States and the EC nations. The United States has by far the smallest percentage of unemployed workers who are long term (defined here as twelve months or more). Although part of the difference in the percentages across nations is due to differences in underlying economic conditions, the U.S. percentages are in fact much lower than those in Germany and Portugal, nations that had roughly the same standardized (to match the United States definition) unemployment rate in 1989. While there are many factors that influence durations of unemployment across nations, including the nature of their unemployment insurance systems (see chapter 5), the structure of health insurance may also be a contributing factor.

19. Gruber and Madrian (1993); Monheit and Cooper (1993); Cooper and Monheit (forthcoming); Holtz-Eakin (1992); Madrian (1992); Olson (1993).

20. I owe this point to John Abowd. Under the Comprehensive Omnibus Budget Reconciliation Act of 1985, workers laid off by large American employers are eligible to continue their health insurance coverage for up to eighteen months if they pay the entire premium plus a 2 percent surcharge. Flynn (1992). Because of the high costs of health insurance, many unemployed workers choose not to exercise this option.

Table 3-8. *Long-Term Unemployment as a Percent of Total Unemployment in the United States and EC Nations for Men and Women Aged 25–54, 1989* [a]
Percent

Country	Men	Women	Standardized unemployment rate
Belgium	82.5	82.5	8.0
Denmark	26.0	34.3	n.a.
France	43.2	48.5	9.4
Germany	55.5	47.2	5.6
Greece	46.5	36.2	n.a.
Ireland	76.1	63.7	15.6
Italy	66.3	71.8	10.9
Netherlands	69.3	51.2	8.3
Portugal	46.3	57.1	5.0
Spain	53.1	67.9	16.9
United Kingdom	55.1	28.7	7.1
United States	9.9	4.6	5.2

Source: For first 2 columns, *OECD Employment Outlook, July 1992,* table 5.10; for last column, ibid., table T.

n.a. Not available.

a. Long-term unemployment is defined as unemployment of twelve months or more.

Chapter 4

Employment Standards

A LMOST all nations establish employment standards, or minimal conditions under which they believe individuals should be employed. Examples are minimum wage and maximum hours laws, child labor and compulsory schooling laws, occupational safety and health laws, equal employment or antidiscrimination laws, and laws governing the conditions under which workers can be dismissed (discussed in the next chapter).

Critics of free trade argue that it is both an immoral act and unfair competition for the United States to make a free trade agreement with a nation that has much lower employment standards than we do or fails to enforce its existing standards. In the debate that preceded the passage of NAFTA in 1993, some opponents argued that the treaty should not be signed unless side agreements were established to guarantee Mexico's adherence to its own standards in the areas of, among others, minimum wages, child labor law, and occupational safety and health.[1] The sections that follow focus on these three types of employment standards, present some information about their nature and variation, and discuss the relationship between them and the ability of economies to integrate more fully.

Before doing so, I want to stress that employment standards usually impose costs on employers that they cannot fully shift onto employees. For example, a minimum wage law that sets the minimum wage at a level above that which would prevail in the absence of the law will raise the cost of low-skilled workers unless employers can compensatingly reduce employee benefit levels.[2] Similarly, child labor laws, by restricting the

---

1. The Clinton administration negotiated such a side agreement in August of 1993. For details see "How Complaints Would Be Handled," *New York Times,* August 14, 1993, p. 45, and chapter 7.

2. For empirical evidence on the ability of employers to reduce benefits in response to minimum wage increases, see Wessels (1981).

supply of young low-skilled workers, will increase the wage levels employers must pay to employ low-skilled workers. Finally, if the value employees place on the improved occupational safety and health that result from occupational safety and health legislation is less than employers' costs of complying with the legislation, only part of the costs will be shifted onto employees in the form of lower wages, and employers' costs will again rise.[3]

In each case, the impact of the employment standard on employers' costs will vary among employers. Minimum wage laws will increase costs the most for employers who have production processes that make the most use of low-skilled workers. Child labor laws will increase costs the most for the same group of employers. Occupational safety and health legislation will affect employers' costs the most when health and safety conditions are initially poor and major expenditures are required to comply with the legislation.

As regards minimum wage and child labor legislation, suppose that many developing nations, such as Mexico, have a comparative advantage (relative to the United States) in producing goods that use low-skilled, labor-intensive production processes. To the extent that minimum wage and child labor standards raise the costs of goods that are produced using low-skilled, labor-intensive production processes, U.S. employers of low-skilled labor will be placed at a competitive disadvantage if foreign producers are not subject to similar standards.

Following the logic used in chapter 1, where the effect of a payroll tax with a relatively low taxable wage base was discussed, the comparative advantage of foreign producers of goods that are made using low-skilled, labor-intensive production methods will be decreased and fewer of these goods imported when foreign low-skilled workers are covered by such standards, as compared with when they are not. Put another way, the demand for U.S. low-skilled workers will be higher when foreign low-skilled workers are subject to such standards.

Not surprisingly, then, employers who make heavy use of low-skilled labor and the unions representing these workers are often among the chief opponents of free trade agreements, such as NAFTA. They are also likely to be among the chief proponents of requiring potential trading partners to adopt similar standards as ours *and* of requiring foreign nations to ensure compliance with their own standards.

---

3. The reasoning behind this statement is analogous to that used in figure 3-1, which illustrates that if the cost to employers of health insurance exceeds the value employees place on the insurance, only part of the cost can be shifted onto employees.

Table 4-1. *Minimum Wages in Selected Countries, October 1992*

Country	System
North America	
Canada	Statutory minimum wage (by province)
Mexico	Statutory minimum wage
United States	Statutory minimum wage (federal and state)
Europe	
Austria	Legally binding, industry level agreements
Belgium (EC)	Legally binding, national central agreement
Cyprus	Not legally binding, sectoral agreements, selective statutory minima
Denmark (EC)	Legally binding, sectoral agreements
Finland	Legally binding, sectoral agreements
France (EC)	Statutory minimum wage
Germany (EC)	Legally binding, sectoral agreements
Greece (EC)	Legally binding, national central agreement
Ireland (EC)	Selective sectoral statutory minima
Italy (EC)	Legally binding, industry level agreements
Luxembourg (EC)	Statutory minimum wage
Malta	Statutory minimum wage
Netherlands (EC)	Statutory minimum wage
Portugal (EC)	Statutory minimum wage
Spain (EC)	Statutory minimum wage
Sweden	Legally binding, industry level agreements
Switzerland	Industry level agreements
United Kingdom (EC)	Selective statutory sectoral minima

Source: "Minimum Pay in 18 Countries" (1992).

Minimum Wages

Table 4-1 presents information on minimum wages in a set of North American and European countries. In some countries the minimum wage is statutorily set at the national level (for example, in France). In other countries it is set regionally by lower levels of government (for example, by province in Canada). In still other countries it is determined by legally binding collective bargaining agreements at either the national (as in Belgium) or sector-industry level (as in Sweden), or by non-legally binding agreements (as in Cyprus). Finally, the United States has both a legally binding national minimum wage and individual state minimum wages. The latter are typically equal to or less than the national minimum; their purpose is to extend coverage to workers not covered by the federal law. But in a few states, such as California and New Jersey, the state minimum has at times exceeded the federal minimum.

Because of differences in real income levels, one would not expect the nominal value of the minimum wage to be equal either across countries or across areas within a country. One might expect, however, that in countries where minimum wages were set regionally, the minimum wage would roughly equal the same proportion of the average wage in each area. That this does not always occur is evident from Canada, where, in early 1993, the minimum wage as a percent of average earnings varied from 43 to 52 percent across provinces.[4] In the United States, with its uniform national minimum wage, the variation is even more dramatic. In January 1993 the national minimum wage as a share of average hourly earnings in manufacturing varied among states from 28 percent in Michigan to 47 percent in Mississippi.[5]

The variation in the ratio of the minimum wage to average earnings that exists across provinces in Canada and states in the United States, a variation that has persisted over long periods, suggests that increased international economic integration will not, in itself, cause the relative values of minimum wages to converge across countries. Whether requiring that they do should become a precondition for increased integration is discussed below.

Minimum Wage Legislation in the United States

A brief survey of the history of minimum wage laws in the United States and a discussion of some of their effects will shed light on how international economic integration will influence, and be influenced by, minimum wage laws. Minimum wages at the federal level in the United States began with the passage of the Fair Labor Standards Act in 1938. The FLSA initially covered only workers involved in interstate trade, primarily those in manufacturing and mining. The minimum wage was first set at 25 cents an hour, which was approximately 40 percent of average hourly earnings in manufacturing in 1938.[6] Since 1938 changes have periodically been made to the nominal minimum wage to adjust for growth in the general level of wages and prices.

Coverage has also expanded over time; as new low-wage industries (such as retail trade) or low-wage areas (such as Puerto Rico) have

4. Unpublished data provided to the author by the Ontario Ministry of Treasury and Economics, Ottawa.

5. In January 1993, when the national minimum wage was $4.25 an hour, average hourly earnings in manufacturing were $9.06 in Mississippi and $15.00 in Michigan. See U.S. Department of Labor (1993a, table C-8).

6. Ehrenberg and Smith (1994, table 3-3).

become covered, the minimum wage has been phased in slowly to try to avoid disruptions that sudden large increases in labor costs might cause. As manufacturing decreased in importance and coverage was expanded to lower-wage industries, the standard of reference for the minimum wage increasingly became average hourly earnings in the entire private nonagricultural sector, not simply average hourly earnings in manufacturing. As a result, the ratio of the minimum wage to average hourly earnings in manufacturing has trended downward somewhat over the last thirty years.

In spite of the expansion in coverage, in 1990 about 12 percent of nonsupervisory employees were not covered, because of the exclusion of some employees in agriculture, wholesale and retail trade, finance insurance and real estate, and the service industries.[7] Since many of these employees work for small firms whose annual sales fall below specified limits, they are not subject to minimum wage regulations.

The 1989 amendments to the FLSA temporarily introduced a youth differential into U.S. minimum wage legislation.[8] They provided that young people aged sixteen to nineteen in their first six months of employment on their first job could be paid a youth differential, or training wage, of approximately 85 percent of the nominal minimum wage. The youth differential provision was subject to a "sunset clause," and it expired on March 31, 1993.

As mentioned, many states have their own state minimum wage laws. In some, these laws cover only workers not covered by the federal minimum wage and provide these workers with a minimum wage that is less than or equal to the federal minimum wage. Other states have specified state minimum wages for all workers that at times have exceeded the federal minimum wages.[9]

Studies of compliance with minimum wage laws in the United States show that a substantial proportion of the low-wage workers who should legally be receiving at least the minimum wage receive lower wage rates. Indeed, estimates of noncompliance as high as 35 to 45 percent have been reported in the literature.[10] High noncompliance rates are not surprising, given the low level of resources devoted to enforcing compliance with the FLSA and the small penalties faced by identified first

7. U.S. Department of Labor (1993b, table 7).
8. In fact, a youth differential for some students had existed for many years; the 1989 law applied to all teenagers.
9. For example, California set its state minimum wage at $4.25 an hour in July of 1988, at a time that the federal minimum was still $3.35.
10. Ashenfelter and Smith (1979). Other analysts use a different definition of noncompliance and come up with smaller rates. See Sellekaerts and Welch (1984); Sellekaerts and Welch (1983).

offenders.[11] The literature does suggest, however, that compliance with the FLSA is higher whenever there are unions that can monitor firms' behavior and report violations to the government.[12]

A growing body of evidence suggests that the negative effects of increases in the minimum wage on employment are small or zero in the United States.[13] This reflects the "unimportance" of minimum wage increases when both the minimum is low relative to prevailing wage levels in the economy and only a small proportion of workers are receiving the minimum. In contrast, recent research on the extension of the minimum wage to Puerto Rico suggests that increases in minimum wages have much larger negative effects on employment when both the minimum is set high relative to prevailing wage levels and a large proportion of workers are receiving the minimum.[14]

Minimum Wages and Economic Integration

Should the minimum wage be set at the same nominal level across nations? Part of the gains from trade and economic integration comes about when nations can profit from international differences in comparative advantage that exist because of differences in nations' endowments of technology, capital, skilled labor, unskilled labor, and other inputs. To require the minimum to be equal in all nations would artificially raise costs and reduce the comparative advantage of nations with relatively large supplies of unskilled labor and thus would reduce the benefits from free trade.

What level of the minimum wage might a nation want to require of its trading partners? Some argue that the failure to require any minimum standard will lead to unfair competition, the exploitation of workers abroad, and ultimately a decline in a nation's own minimum wage standard as the nation seeks to keep jobs from fleeing abroad. Others argue, however, that attempts to require trading partners to increase their minimum wages do not reflect concern for the welfare of workers

11. The Wages and Hours Division of the U.S. Department of Labor is responsible for enforcing all the provisions of the FLSA (minimum wage, overtime premium, and child labor) plus other wage-related statutes. In fiscal 1989 the department employed fewer than 1,000 compliance officers nationwide and inspected only 1.5 percent of all establishments covered by the FLSA. See U.S. General Accounting Office (1990, p. 2).

12. Ehrenberg and Schumann (1982).

13. Katz and Krueger (1992); Card (1992a); Card (1992b); Neumark and Wascher (1982).

14. Castillo-Freeman and Freeman (1991); Castillo-Freeman and Freeman (1992, pp. 177–212). Similar evidence on the effects of relatively high French minimum wages is presented in Bazen and Martin (1991).

abroad, but are really protectionist attempts to preserve employment at home.[15]

The EC nations have agreed not to address the issue directly. Article 8 of the European Social Charter asserts that workers have the right to earn an equitable wage that is sufficient for them to have a decent standard of living.[16] But the setting of wages within each country is deemed to be a matter for that country alone. Because the variation in real wages across the EC nations was not large before the entry of Greece, Portugal, and Spain in the 1980s, the setting of minimum wage levels was simply not an important issue in the European policy debate.

In contrast, average wage differences between the United States and Mexico are enormous.[17] Thus the debate over NAFTA involved considerable discussion about the appropriate level of the Mexican minimum wage. Some argued that before NAFTA was signed, Mexico should have been required to set its minimum wage as a specified fraction of its own average wage. How this fraction would have been determined is unclear, given the wide variation in the comparable fractions already noted in the Canadian provinces and U.S. states.

Others argued that Mexican wages had been kept artificially low by the Mexican government and that average Mexican wages were therefore an irrelevant reference point. This group wanted the minimum to be set relative to some measure of Mexican productivity such as the value added per worker in export industries.[18] The idea of tying the minimum to some trade-related measure has some precedent—as noted earlier, the minimum wage in the United States was originally set with reference to average wages in industries involved in interstate trade. Critics of such proposals, however, note that productivity in export industries often rises faster than productivity in nontraded goods and thus that such proposals might cause the minimum to perpetually rise relative to average wages in the economy.

Although proponents of a higher minimum would allow it to be phased in over time, the fact remains that when the minimum wage is set high relative to current wages and a large share of workers earn the minimum, the higher minimum wage is likely to cause substantial em-

15. A similar argument has been used to explain why unions that represent relatively high-paid workers are often among the strongest proponents of higher federal or state minimum wages. See, for example, Cox and Oaxaca (1981).

16. "Minimum Pay in 18 Countries" (1992).

17. In 1992 average hourly compensation costs for production workers in manufacturing were $16.17 in the United States but only $2.35 in Mexico. See Anthony DePalma, "Law Protects Mexico's Workers but Its Enforcement Is Often Lax," *New York Times*, August 14, 1993, p. 1.

18. Rothstein (1993).

ployment losses.[19] Thus many of the very people whom proponents allege they are trying to help—namely, low-wage Mexican workers in the case of NAFTA—would be hurt, although those who kept their jobs would obviously be better off. American consumers would also be hurt, since higher Mexican minimum wages would reduce Mexico's comparative advantage in producing goods using unskilled labor and so would reduce the benefits to the United States from importing Mexican goods.

If minimum wages were to be specified for a trading partner, would agreement on exemptions also be sought? Could the trading partner have a youth differential such as the United States recently had, and if so, is the 15 percent "discount" employers were permitted to pay new teenage workers for six months in the United States, the only discount that would be permissible? The United States has historically exempted small employers from much of its protective labor legislation and employment standards because of the fear that adding costs onto these employers' backs might cause them to go out of business.[20] Would the United States permit its trading partners to have similar, or even more widespread, exemptions for their small employers?

The monitoring and enforcement of compliance is also an issue that raises a host of questions. In the United States there is substantial noncompliance with minimum wage laws because the resources it devotes to monitoring compliance are low, as are the penalties for noncompliance if caught. Should the United States require trading partners to devote more resources to monitoring compliance and have higher penalties for noncompliance than it does? Since one important role unions play is to help monitor and enforce compliance with standards, should the United States encourage the growth of strong unions in its trading partners? Would such encouragement seem hypocritical, given

19. Rothstein argues that in an analogous low-wage economic environment the gradual imposition of high (U.S.) minimum wage levels in Puerto Rico was associated with high growth rates in real per capita personal income. How can one reconcile that statement with Castillo-Freeman and Freeman's evidence (cited earlier) that this action caused substantial employment losses in Puerto Rico? One answer given by the latter is that Puerto Ricans are free to legally migrate to mainland United States and legally do so. By 1980 one-third of all people aged 20 to 64 who were born in Puerto Rico were residing in the U.S. mainland. Although real wages did grow in Puerto Rico by 174 percent during 1951–88, Castillo-Freeman and Freeman estimated that these gains would have been reduced by one-quarter if the emigrants had remained in Puerto Rico and increased the island's labor supply. The implication one might draw from the Puerto Rican experience is that if increases in the Mexican minimum wage reduced Mexican employment opportunities, this might lead to substantial increases in illegal immigration to the United States.

20. For example, such exemptions for small employers exist in the Fair Labor Standards Act minimum wage and overtime pay provisions, in advance notice for plant shutdown legislation, and in the recently passed Family and Medical Leave Act.

the decline of private sector unionism in the United States (discussed in chapter 6)?

Further, should a bilateral or a multilateral agency be established with a large staff to monitor and investigate compliance in both the United States and its trading partners, and then deny a company the right to take advantage of free trade provisions for a specified time if it is caught not complying? Would such infringements on national sovereignty be acceptable to any of the parties? Should the United States instead require firms to be certified by investigators from their home country that they are complying with minimum wage laws before they are permitted to take advantage of free trade provisions? If so, should a poor country like Mexico finance its compliance enforcement efforts through a "tax" on its exports? Does compliance today imply that firms would comply tomorrow? Would the United States even accept at face value the certifications from a foreign country?

Under the actual labor-side agreements to NAFTA, which were approved in 1993, nations are responsible for enforcing their own laws. If a nation fails to do so and refuses to develop a satisfactory enforcement plan, fines of up to $20 million can be imposed on the nation, and its trade privileges can be modified or revoked by representatives from Canada, Mexico, and the United States. Whether this system has any chance of succeeding is discussed in chapter 7.

Compulsory Schooling and Child Labor Laws

Recognizing the importance of education to a person's lifetime well-being and to the economic productivity of a country, most nations require youths to attend school until a certain age. In the United States and Canada the compulsory schooling age is 16; in Mexico and Japan, it is 14 and 15, respectively (table 4-2).[21] Compulsory schooling ages vary widely across the EC and other European nations, ranging from 13 in Italy to 18 in Belgium and Germany.

To encourage young people to remain enrolled in school, to discourage their considering employment as an option to schooling, and to protect them from hazardous working conditions, most nations also set minimum ages at which youths may be employed and limit the number of hours those enrolled in school may work. For example, the minimum age for regular employment varies across the EC nations from 14 in

21. Compulsory schooling ages are determined at the state level in the United States and vary from a low of 14 (Mississippi) to a high of 18 in a number of states. See National Center for Education Statistics (1992, table 142).

Table 4-2. *Compulsory Schooling Ages and Minimum Ages for Employment in Selected Countries, 1990*

Country	Compulsory school required until age	Minimum age for employment	Minimum age for employment	
			Light work[a]	Dangerous work[b]
Canada	16	Varies	. . .	16–18
Japan	15	15	12	18
United States	16	16	. . .	16–18
Mexico	14	14	. . .	16
Belgium (EC)	18	14	. . .	16–21
Denmark (EC)	15	15	10–13	16–18
France (EC)	16	16	12–14	16–18
Germany (EC)	18	15	13	18
Greece (EC)	15	15	. . .	16–18
Ireland (EC)	15	15	14	18
Italy (EC)	13	14–15	14	15–18
Luxembourg (EC)	15	15	. . .	18
Netherlands (EC)	16	15	13–15	18
Norway	15	15	13	18
Portugal (EC)	14	15	15	18
Spain (EC)	15	16	. . .	16–18
Sweden	16	16	13	18
Switzerland	15	15	13	16–18
United Kingdom (EC)	16	13–16	. . .	16–18

Source: International Labour Office (1991, annex 1).

a. Light work is work that is not likely to be harmful to a child's health and that will not prejudice the child's attendance at school.

b. Dangerous work is work that is likely to jeopardize the health, safety, or morals of a young person.

Belgium to 16 in France and Spain (table 4-2). Often part-time work in certain jobs that will not interfere with school and are not harmful to health (light work) is permitted at an earlier age, whereas work in more dangerous occupations is often not permitted until a later age.

Do these laws serve their intended purposes? Recent research suggests that as many as 25 percent of potential dropouts in the United States remain in school because of compulsory schooling laws and that these young people reap a substantial economic return for their "forced" extra schooling.[22] In contrast, compliance with child labor laws does not appear to be high in the United States. In fiscal year

22. Angrist and Krueger (1991).

1989 the Department of Labor, which devotes few resources to monitoring compliance, detected about 22,000 violations of federal child labor law regulations.[23] A separate study by the General Accounting Office estimated, however, that in calendar year 1988 about 18 percent of all employed 15-year-olds, or 166,000 youths, were working in violation of federal legislation governing maximum hours or minimum ages of employment for youths.[24]

The (mis)use of child labor in Mexico was raised repeatedly by opponents of NAFTA during the policy debate. They argued that NAFTA should not have been signed unless it was accompanied by side agreements that guaranteed both stricter child labor law standards in Mexico and the enforcement of the standards. The side agreements adopted call for stricter enforcement but do not address the level at which the standards should be set. The failure of the United States to devote sufficient resources to generate widespread compliance with its own child labor standards leads to concerns that demanding enforcement of such standards by a trading partner may not only be hypocritical but also require more resources than the trading partner can devote to the task.

As noted in the previous section, generating revenue to cover the costs of enforcing standards through a "tax" on exports is one way to address the issue. In effect, this would be a tariff (which the free trade agreements were seeking to reduce), with the revenue going to the national government for the explicit purpose of enforcement. More generally, all the issues raised in the previous section would be applicable here.

Occupational Safety and Health Standards

The establishment of federal safety and health standards that covered most employees did not occur in the United States until the passage of the Occupational Safety and Health Act (OSHA) in 1970. Before then, a few hazardous industries with high injury rates, for example, maritime, were subject to federal regulations, and a number of states had their own regulations.

Enforcement of the standards set under the act has varied over time.[25] Initially some inspections were spread over all employers, and some were targeted at industries with high injury rates. In 1977 inspection effort was redirected toward large firms, with a focus on more serious hazards. In

23. U.S. General Accounting Office (1990).
24. U.S. General Accounting Office (1991, pp. 4–5).
25. U.S. Department of Labor (1993c).

1980 small firms in low-injury rate industries were exempted from programmed inspections. A movement was also begun toward "records inspections," in which compliance officers would first check an establishment's injury-rate records and then formally inspect the work site only if the establishment's injury rate was above the national average. Because, as was eventually realized, this provided firms with incentives to underreport injury rates, records inspections were terminated in 1990. Throughout, inspections could also be initiated by a worker or union complaint, and if a serious violation was found at a work site, a reinspection often took place to ensure that a hazardous condition had been remedied. In recent years the number of compliance safety and health officers available to undertake inspections has ranged between 1,100 and 1,200 nationwide.[26]

OSHA violations are classified as *serious, other than serious, repeat, failure to abate,* and *willful.* Serious violations are those for which there is a substantial probability that death or serious harm could result from the violation. Other-than-serious violations are those that present somewhat less risk to workers. Repeat, failure to abate, and willful (an intentional and knowing act) violations can be either serious or other than serious, although in practice they tend to be the former. The average penalties for serious, willful, repeat, and failure-to-abate violations were $484, $13,129, $1,556, and $3,188, respectively, in fiscal 1991, even though the penalty provisions of OSHA provide for potentially much larger fines.[27] For example, the maximum penalty for a willful violation was set at $10,000 in the original act and raised to $70,000 in 1990.

In fiscal 1991 more than 42,000 workplaces were inspected in the United States and more than 153,000 violations were found. Over two-thirds of these violations were classified as serious, willful, repeat, or failure to abate.[28] Recognizing that the establishments inspected are not a random sample of establishments in the United States, it is still true that, on average, more than two of these more important kinds of violations were found per inspection.

The final striking piece of evidence is that since the passage of OSHA there has been no discernible trend in workplace injury rates in the United States. For example, the share of manufacturing workers experiencing lost workday injuries was 4.0 percent in 1972, but averaged 5.3 percent during the 1988–90 period. Although questions remain about the changing accuracy of injury-rate data over time, a careful review of the raw data and of the academic literature concluded that in the aggre-

26. U.S. Department of Labor (1993c, table 6).
27. U.S. Department of Labor (1993c, table 4).
28. U.S. Department of Labor (1993c, tables 1, 4).

gate injury rates seem to have been unaffected by OSHA. Similarly, the review suggested that the inspection process per se has had at most a small effect on injury rates.[29]

What are the implications of these findings for economic integration? First, the observation that the occupational safety and health standards adopted by a wealthy developed nation appear to have had little effect on injury rates does not imply that standards enacted and enforced in a developing nation would be ineffective there. Wealthier nations tend to have better working conditions than poorer ones in several areas (shorter hours, fewer injuries), because workers in the former have "taken" some of their increased productivity in the form of better working conditions rather than solely in the form of increased wages. Poorer nations tend to have poorer working conditions; thus the potential for standards that are enforced to improve worker safety and health is much higher in them.[30] As a result, the labor side agreements to NAFTA *do* require Mexico to enforce its own occupational safety and health standards.

However, if U.S. standards and how the United States enforces them keep evolving, if the resources it devotes to ensuring compliance are low, if the penalties it assigns for noncompliance are small, and if instances of noncompliance (at least as measured by violations per inspection) are high, how can the United States justify mandating standards or compliance levels for its trading partners, especially if these are developing nations? Moreover, if improved working conditions are a byproduct of economic development, can the United States reasonably demand that poorer countries set the same level of standards or devote as many resources to enforcing compliance as it does?

The question arises again: should the United States be willing to bear some of the cost of improving working conditions in its poorer trading partners through, in this case, a "safety and health standard" tariff? But, would not doing so decrease the gains to trade to American consumers? Alternatively, should the United States provide funding to help improve its trading partners' workplace safety and health out of a nontrade-related source, such as general federal tax revenues. Such a policy would not, as a safety and health standard tariff would, restrict trade by altering relative prices; thus it would not directly save jobs in trade-competing industries as a social (some might argue protectionist) tariff would. Taxpayers as a whole, however, would see their net gains from trade reduced, for their disposable income would be reduced. Furthermore,

29. Smith (1992).

30. Of course, the health and safety gains from establishing and enforcing standards may at least be partially offset by health losses associated with the poorer nutrition that might result from fewer jobs being created (because of the costs of the standards).

such a funding scheme might not even be feasible, because the projected gains from increased economic integration are often much greater for less-developed nations, such as Mexico, than they are for the United States.[31]

When a nation and its potential trading partners are at roughly the same stage of economic development, as the original set of EC nations were, there is much more room for common agreement about minimal occupational safety and health standards. Besides taking into account worker well-being, such standards also serve to prevent employers from social dumping (in this case locating in countries where health and safety protection is less developed). The EC, however, aims to do more than harmonize existing minimal standards; it aims to improve worker protection.[32]

Many EC directives relate to workplace safety and health.[33] Although initially these directives set specific standards to reduce specific workplace hazards, increasingly they tend to establish more general obligations. For example, directive 90/394, which deals with the protection of workers from the risks related to exposure to carcinogens on the job, calls for employers to reduce the use of carcinogens in workplaces as much as is technically possible (article 4), and if that is not sufficient, to reduce worker exposure as much as possible (article 5), but the directive does not specify the maximum specific exposure levels that are permissible.[34] Member states are required to establish and enforce the laws necessary to comply with the directive by December 31, 1992 (article 19), but how a nation could enforce such an ambiguous set of requirements is unclear.

The EC experience suggests that whenever trading partners are roughly at the same stage of development and share similar social objectives, establishing standards for occupational safety and health as part of a multilateral free trade agreement is possible and may facilitate integration. Whether employers widely comply with these standards, especially in the newer, poorer members of the EC (such as Greece, Spain, and Portugal), is unclear.

Occupational safety and health standards can take three forms. The first kind are *criteria* standards, which specify the technology of production that must be used to improve workplace safety or health. For example, a particular piece of safety equipment must be installed on a machine. From an efficiency perspective, economists find such standards

---

31. The point that Mexico will gain much more from NAFTA than the United States will is made by Susan Collins in her forthcoming Brookings book in this series, which deals with distributive issues and economic integration.

32. Holmstedt (1991, pp. 119–28).

33. For a detailed description of each, see European Information Services (1990, pp. 195–565); for an update, "Social Charter State of Play" (1992).

34. European Information Services (1990, pp. 565–79).

lacking, because they do not allow employers to reduce workplace injuries in the most efficient manner.

The second kind are *performance* standards, which specify the maximal level of a "bad" that is permitted. For example, a worker's exposure to noise must not exceed a specified level per day. Such standards allow employers to choose a cost-minimizing way of achieving a standard. In the noise level case, for instance, they can alter the production technology in different ways, provide workers with protective headgears, or rotate workers and limit the time anyone is near noisy equipment. However, when performance standards are established at the same absolute levels for all employers, they will not minimize the costs of achieving a given total level of reduction in exposure unless the marginal cost of achieving the standard is the same across all employers.

The third kind are what I call *expressions* standards, such as those promulgated in EC directive 90/394, which seem more like expressions of good intention than serious standards; because of their imprecision, compliance with them is difficult to monitor. Whether these will have any effect on workers' occupational safety and health is doubtful.

EC directives on workers' safety and health began in the mid-1970s and are a combination of criteria, performance, and expressions standards. Although fatal occupational accident rates have trended downward in many EC nations since the early 1970s, many observers attribute the decline to improved emergency medical services, changes in industry mix, automation, and the increased technical sophistication of equipment, which makes it easier to include safety devices.[35] The increase in real earnings of workers has also led to an increase in their demand for workplace safety. Whether EC directives per se have had any effect on accident rates or whether any reduction in accident rates simply reflects changing worker consumption patterns (increased safety) as real incomes grew is an open question. In other words, the harmonization of occupational safety and health standards by establishing minimal levels that all countries in the EC must meet may have been a necessary political condition to achieve economic integration. However, the benefits from the harmonization of these standards may have come only from the real income growth that economic integration permitted, not from any reduction in injury rates caused by the standards or their enforcement per se.

35. *OECD Employment Outlook, July 1989*, pp. 137–42.

Chapter 5

Policies to Facilitate Labor Market Adjustments

M OST developed nations have policies to facilitate labor market adjustments and to partially compensate workers who become displaced from their jobs. The most common are unemployment insurance; more general income support and welfare programs; training programs and programs to facilitate job placement; legally mandated, collectively bargained, or voluntary employer-provided advance notice of potential job loss; and severance pay for job loss. The importance of these programs increases as international economic integration increases, and they may be essential if governments wish to gain widespread political support for continued greater increased economic integration.

Advance Notice of and Severance Pay for Job Displacement

The Worker Adjustment and Retraining Notification Act (WARN) was passed in the United States in 1988.[1] WARN requires firms with 100 or more employees to provide workers, the state government dislocated-worker unit, and local government officials with written notice sixty days before a planned shutdown or large-scale layoff. The latter is defined as a layoff planned to last at least six months that involves either 500 or more workers or at least one-third of the employer's work force.

Coverage is not universal, however. Besides not covering small firms, the law exempts larger firms from the advance notice requirement for many reasons: for example, if the firm is actively seeking ways to avoid the shutdown (such as trying to find a buyer for the business), if business circumstances that could not be "reasonably foreseen" force the disloca-

1. This section draws heavily on Ehrenberg and Jakubson (1990), and Ehrenberg and Jakubson (1988).

tion (however, notice is required at that point), if a natural disaster directly causes the shutdown or mass layoff, if the firm reallocates within a "reasonable" commuting distance of its previous site and offers employees jobs at the new location, if the workers to be displaced were hired with the understanding that their employment was limited to the duration of a particular project, or if a planned layoff of fewer than sixty days is extended because of "unforeseeable" circumstances. In each of these cases, the burden of proof is on the employer to show that an exemption is warranted.

Penalties for failure to provide the required advance notice include back pay and benefits for each displaced worker for each day of violation and a fine of $500 a day for failing to notify the local government. The law is designed to be enforced through law suits filed in a federal district court by employees, a union, or a local government. Unlike other forms of labor market regulation, such as the Fair Labor Standards Act (FLSA) and the Occupational Safety and Health Act (OSHA), the U.S. Department of Labor has no enforcement authority under WARN. As discussed in the previous chapter, compliance with the FLSA and OSHA is not particularly high.

Most European nations have legislation requiring employers to notify employees about to be laid off or fired (table 5-1). The length of notice necessary typically depends on whether the individual is a white-collar or blue-collar employee and on his or her prior length of service with the firm. The advance notice required in these countries ranges from one week to twenty-four months. When large-scale layoffs or plant shutdowns are contemplated, European law also usually requires firms to notify unions and government and to work with employees and government representatives to attempt to avert the displacement. Often European law requires severance pay (table 5-1). In many European countries small establishments with fewer than twenty employees are exempt from advance notice requirements, perhaps because imposing additional costs on small businesses (which typically have high failure rates) would be a burden, or because a failure of a small business does not have a large negative effect on a community.

Other exemptions also exist under the European legislation. For example, three nations—Ireland, Italy, and the United Kingdom—exempt part-time workers from notification or severance pay requirements. Other nations also do not cover, or only partially cover, part-time workers under their social insurance schemes (table 5-2).

The percent of part-time employees in the work force varies widely across the European nations (table 5-3), and not surprisingly many of the nations that make heavy use of part-time employees (such as Denmark,

Table 5-1. *Requirements for Advance Notice and Severance Pay for Collective Dismissals in European Legislation, 1989*[a]

Country	Definition of collective dismissals	Notice requirement	Severance pay
Austria	Within a 4-week period 5% of work force in ≥ 100 employee firms 50 workers in ≥ 1,000 employee firms	4 weeks	2–12 months salary, based on seniority for employees with ≥3 years tenure
Belgium (EC)	Within a 60-day period 10 employees in 21–99 employee firms 10% of work force in 100–299 employee firms 30 employees in ≥ 300 employee firms	7 days to 15 months, based on occupation and tenure	No requirement
Denmark (EC)	Within a 30-day period 10 employees in 21–99 employee firms 10% of work force in 100–299 employee firms 30 employees in ≥ 300 employee firms	0–6 months, based on occupation and tenure	1–3 months salary, based on seniority for white-collar workers with ≥ 12 years of tenure
Finland	All dismissals for lack of work	2–6 months, based on tenure	No requirement
France (EC)	Within a 30-day period, 2 or more Within a 90-day period, 10 or more employees if ≥ 50 employees	0–2 months, based on tenure	One-tenth of a month of salary per year of tenure if tenure ≥ 2 years
Germany (EC)	Within a 30-day period 5 employees in 21–59 employee firms 25 employees or 10% of the work force in 60–499 employee firms At least 30 employees in ≥ 500 employee firms	2 weeks to 6 months, based on occupation and tenure	No requirement
Greece (EC)	Within a 6-month period 5 employees in 20–50 employee firms 2% of work force in ≥ 50 employee firms	1–24 months, based on tenure	One-half of length of notice period
Ireland (EC)	Within a 30-day period 5 employees in 20–49 employee firms 10 employees in 50–99 employee firms 10% of work force in 100–299 employee firms 30 employees in ≥ 500 employee firms	1–8 weeks, based on tenure	Based on age and tenure if tenure ≥ 2 years

Table 5-1 (*continued*)

Country	Definition of collective dismissals	Notice requirement	Severance pay
Italy (EC)	No requirement	None	Somewhat less than 1 month's earnings per year of service
Luxembourg (EC)	Within a 30-day period, 10 employees Within a 60-day period, 20 employees	2–6 months	1–12 months, based on occupation and tenure
Netherlands (EC)	Within 3 months, 90 or more employees	1–26 weeks, based on tenure and age	No requirement
Norway	Any dismissal	1–6 months, based on age and service	No requirement
Spain (EC)	2 or more employees	30 days	20 days per year of service up to a maximum of 12 months
Sweden	5 to 25 employees involved 26 to 100 More than 100	2 months 4 months 6 months	
United Kingdom (EC)	More than 1 employee	1–12 weeks, based on years of service	Up to £8,925, based on pay, age, length of service, and loss suffered

Source: Author's interpretation of material in Industrial Relations Services (1989).

the Netherlands, Norway, and the United Kingdom) exempt, or limit coverage of, part-time employees under their social insurance or advance notice requirements. Such exemptions and limitations serve to reduce the cost of part-time employees relative to full-timers and thus encourage their substitution.[2] In contrast, when the United Kingdom passed the Employment Protection Act of 1975, which increased the eligibility of part-time employees for severance payments and maternity benefits, its growth rate of part-time employment slowed down.[3]

Should advance notice legislation be a precondition for increased economic integration? Proponents of such legislation argue that notice facilitates displaced workers' search for alternative employment or additional

2. Evidence that the ratio of part-time to full-time employment is negatively related to the ratio of part-time to full-time cost across U.S. industries is presented in Ehrenberg, Rosenberg, and Li (1988, pp. 256–81).

3. Disney and Szyszczak (1984).

Table 5-2. *Coverage of Part-Time Employees under Social Insurance and Dismissal Statutes, Selected European Nations, 1990*

Country	Coverage of part-time employees	
	Notice period and redundancy pay	*Social insurance*
Austria	Yes	Minimum earnings test for sick pay, pension, and unemployment insurance
Belgium (EC)	Yes	Yes
Denmark (EC)	Yes	Must work > 15 hours a week
Finland	Yes	Yes
France (EC)	Yes	Minimum earnings threshold for each type of insurance
Germany (EC)	Yes	Pensions: must work ≥ 15 hours a week must work > 50 days a year Unemployment ins.: must work ≥ 18 hours a week
Greece (EC)	Yes	Yes
Ireland (EC)	Must work > 18 hours a week	Must work ≥ 18 hours a week
Italy (EC)	No	Yes
Luxembourg (EC)	Yes	Unemployment ins.: must work ≥ 18 hours a week
Netherlands (EC)	Yes	Unemployment ins.: must work ≥ 8 hours a week
Norway	Yes	Minimum earnings test for full social security benefits
Portugal (EC)	Yes	Yes
Spain (EC)	Yes	Yes
Sweden	Yes	Yes
United Kingdom (EC)	Only if weekly hours are ≥ 16 if tenure < 5 years ≥ 8 if tenure > 5 years	Excluded from occupational sick pay and pension schemes

Source: Author's interpretation of material in Industrial Relations Services (1990, pp. 19–27).

training. Notifying government agencies allows them lead time to mobilize their resources to assist displaced workers. Indeed, a companion piece of legislation to WARN, the Economic Dislocation and Worker Adjustment Assistance Act, specifically requires the Department of Labor to fund programs for states to aid dislocated workers and to create dislocated-worker units that counsel workers about alternative employment and new training.

Table 5-3. *The Use of Nonstandard Forms of Employment, 1989, 1990,*
Selected OECD Nations

Country	Part-time employment as a percent of total employment, 1990	Temporary employment as a percent of total employment, 1989
Australia	21.3	n.a.
Austria	8.8[a]	n.a.
Belgium (EC)	10.2[a]	5.1
Canada	15.4	n.a.
Denmark (EC)	23.7[b]	9.9
Finland	7.2	n.a.
France (EC)	12.0	8.5
Germany (EC)	13.2[b]	11.0
Greece (EC)	5.5[b]	17.2
Ireland (EC)	8.1[b]	8.6
Italy (EC)	5.7[a]	6.3
Japan	17.6	10.8
Luxembourg (EC)	6.5[b]	3.4
Netherlands (EC)	33.2	8.5
New Zealand	20.1	n.a.
Norway	26.6	n.a.
Portugal (EC)	5.9[a]	18.7
Spain (EC)	4.8[a]	26.6
Sweden	23.2	n.a.
United Kingdom (EC)	21.8[a]	5.4
United States	16.9	n.a.

Source: *OECD Employment Outlook, July 1991*, tables 2.9 (A), (B).
n.a. not available.
a. Data are for 1989.
b. Data are for 1988.

Advance notice also allows employers, workers, unions, and government to collaborate to determine whether there are ways to prevent the plant closing or layoffs. Such measures might be, for example, wage concessions by the workers, tax concessions by government, the restructuring of the work environment to improve productivity, or a search for new ownership, including employee ownership.

To the extent that advance notice facilitates workers' transition to new jobs or helps to avert workers' displacement, proponents argue, it benefits local communities as well as individual workers. Plant shutdowns and massive layoffs place extra demands on communities for social services, since the stress induced by unemployment causes an increased incidence of physical and mental ailments at the same time that local sales and property tax revenues are reduced.

Opponents of advance notice legislation argue that it will restrict the free mobility of capital, increase worker turnover, and decrease productivity. They also argue that advance notice will decrease the likelihood that buyers of the plant's product will place new orders, that banks will supply new credit, that suppliers will continue to provide services, and that the firm can sell the plant to potential buyers. (The latter explains one of the exemptions under WARN.) In addition, opponents believe that advance notice may depress corporate stock prices, and that by effectively increasing the cost of reducing employment, it can encourage firms to use overtime hours rather than expand employment.[4]

Critics of WARN and similar legislation object to the fact that the advance notice is mandatory. Proponents respond that without mandatory advance notice very few displaced workers will receive such notice; evidence from the United States suggests they are correct on that point.[5]

In evaluating advance notice legislation, it is important to stress that an employer does not bear the full social cost of the plant shutdown or mass layoff. An employer normally does not take into account the costs that a mass layoff or plant shutdown imposes on the community; for example, that the displacement simultaneously decreases the community's revenue base and increases the demand for its social services. Consequently, proponents of advance notice requirements argue that the legislation helps internalize these external costs, and that by implicitly increasing the cost of plant closings or mass layoffs, employers will be discouraged from taking such actions. Meanwhile critics stress that anything that implicitly or explicitly increases labor costs will encourage the flight of jobs overseas. Hence they are implicitly arguing for the harmonization of notice standards across nations.

Because of the limitations of WARN—its myriad exemptions and the possibility of noncompliance—the majority of displaced workers in the United States do not appear to be receiving sixty days' advance notice, even when the law seems to require it.[6] For workers who have received notice, the notice apparently does serve to improve their probability of finding new employment before the layoff date. However, advance notice per se seems to have no effect on displaced workers subsequent earnings or on their duration of unemployment if they become unemployed.[7] Thus, although advance notice may reduce the short-run costs of job

4. Lazear (1990) finds evidence that increases in the generosity of severance pay provisions in an OECD nation were associated with reductions in the nation's employment-population ratio.

5. Ehrenberg and Jakubson (1988, pp. 8–13).

6. U.S. General Accounting Office (1993).

7. See, for example, Ehrenberg and Jakubson (1990, chaps. 5, 6); Swaim and Podgursky (1990); Addison and Portugal (1992).

displacement, in itself it does not reduce the considerable long-run wage losses that displaced workers experience.[8] This suggests that additional adjustment policies will be required to win widespread political support for continued increased economic integration.

Before considering these other policies, it is interesting to note that EC directive 75/129, adopted in February 1975, spells out the minimum notice requirements expected in case of collective redundancies.[9] Collective redundancies are defined as either layoffs during a thirty-day period of 10 or more workers in small (20 to 99 employee) establishments, 10 percent or more of the workers in medium-size (100 to 299 employees) establishments, and 30 or more workers in large (300 or more employees) establishments, or layoffs of 20 or more workers during a ninety-day period *regardless of establishment size.* The directive specifically excludes temporary workers on fixed-term contracts, and calls for a minimum of thirty days' notice, which can be extended to sixty days at the request of the government. Remembering that EC directives are binding on all member nations, this directive specifies compliance within two years (1977) of its adoption.

Although most EC nations have fully complied with the directive, some provide very little notice for relatively low-tenure employees (table 5-1). Moreover, some have excluded or limited coverage of part-time workers (table 5-2). Finally, the specific exemption for temporary employees undoubtedly contributes to the high level of temporary and fixed-term employment in several EC nations, particularly in the relatively poorer nations of Greece, Portugal, and Spain (table 5-3). If directives have loopholes, nations can structure their national legislation to comply with the language of the directives but not necessarily their spirit.

The EC is fully aware of the increased use of part-time and fixed-term employees, and over the years several directives have been proposed to improve the working conditions of such employees, including more fully covering them under collective redundancy laws.[10]

Policies That Partially Compensate for Job Loss

Almost all of the developed nations that belong to the Organization of Economic Cooperation and Development (OECD) provide unemployed workers with some form of income support. The systems that provide

8. Ruhm (1991); Jacobson, LaLonde, and Sullivan (1993).

9. European Information Services (1990, pp. 114–18). The directive was revised in June of 1992, but its essential provisions were not changed. See "Revised Collective Redundancies Directive" (1992).

10. See Industrial Relations Services (1990, pp. 1–13).

Table 5-4. *Selected Characteristics of Unemployment Insurance and Assitance Systems, Selected OECD Nations, January 1989*

Country	Benefit type[a]	Maximum duration	Initial gross replacement rate (percent)[b]
Economic Community			
Belgium	UI	Indefinite	60
Denmark	UI	30 mos.	64
	GI	Indefinite	17
France	UI	30 mos.	59
	UA	Indefinite	26
Germany	UI	12 mos.	58
	UA	Indefinite	52
Greece	UI	5 mos.	50
Ireland	UI	15 mos.	29
	UA	Indefinite	20
Italy	UI	6 mos.	15
Netherlands	UI	36 mos.	70
	GI	Indefinite	40
Portugal	UI	n.a.	60
	UA	15 mos.	40
Spain	UI	24 mos.	62
United Kingdom	UI	12 mos.	16
	GI	Indefinite	16
Other OECD, Europe			
Austria	UI	30 weeks	41
	UA	Indefinite	38
Finland	UI	24 mos.	59
	UA	Indefinite	26
Norway	UI	80 weeks	62
	SW	Indefinite	19
Sweden	UI	60 weeks	90
	SW	Indefinite	27
Switzerland	UI	50 weeks	70
Other OECD, Non-Europe			
Australia	GI	Indefinite	24
Canada[c]	UI	50 weeks	60
	SW	Indefinite	23
Japan	UI	30 weeks	48
New Zeland	GI	Indefinite	27
United States[c]	UI	26 weeks	50

Source: *OECD Employment Outlook, July 1991*, table 7.2.

n.a. Not available.

a. UI: unemployment insurance; GI: guaranteed minimum income; UA: unemployment assistance; SW: social welfare.

b. For a single worker age 40, at average productive worker's 1988 earnings level.

c. The U.S. and Canadian systems vary by state and province, respectively. The numbers in the tables are the estimates of the average value across regions made by the authors of the table in the source.

this support can be roughly categorized into unemployment insurance (UI), unemployment assistance (UA), guaranteed minimum income (GI), and social welfare systems (SW) (table 5-4).[11]

UI systems usually relate benefits to past employment histories; they offer a form of insurance for earnings loss due to unemployment. UA systems provide needs-based benefits (need under them is typically defined at a higher level than it is for GI or SW systems). In many countries, such as Denmark and France, UI and UA systems coexist, and after receiving UI benefits for a predetermined maximum length of time, an unemployed worker would receive UA benefits which are lower if he or she was still unemployed and was judged to have sufficient need. GI and SW systems cover employed as well as unemployed workers. GI systems are nationally based and provide a minimum guaranteed income level, whereas SW systems provide minimum income guarantees that vary locally or regionally.

Table 5-4 contains information on the maximum duration of benefits and the replacement rate that the average manufacturing production worker would receive, when he or she first became eligible for benefits. The generosity of these systems, as measured by the replacement rates, varies widely across nations. For example, whereas many EC nations have initial replacement rates in the 60 percent range or higher (Belgium, Denmark, France, Germany, Netherlands, Portugal, and Spain), several others have initial replacement rates that are below 20 percent (Ireland and the United Kingdom).

Unemployment insurance and assistance systems are much more complicated than the simple specification of benefit levels and the duration of eligibility.[12] They vary, among other ways, in the criteria unemployed workers must meet to initially qualify for benefits (labor market histories, reason for unemployment) and in the criteria they must meet to continue receiving benefits (required efforts to look for suitable work). Because of these variations and the fact that in some countries unemployed workers exhaust their benefits after a predetermined length of time (for example, six months in Italy), not all unemployed workers receive UI at any one time. Indeed, as the following informal table shows, during the late 1980s, 40 percent or less of the unemployed workers in the United States, the United Kingdom, and Germany were receiving unemployment insurance or assistance benefits:[13]

11. "Unemployment Benefit Rules and Labour Market Policy" (1991).

12. See "Unemployment Benefit Rules and Labour Market Policy" (1991); and for details of the U.S. systems, National Foundation for Unemployment Compensation and Workers' Compensation (1993).

13. Estimates of various authors reported in Atkinson and Micklewright (1991, pp. 1689–90).

Country	Year	Percent
United States	1987	<30
Great Britain	1988	26
Germany	1988	40
Sweden	1978–85	60–70

Within North America, the Canadian provincial UI systems are usually more generous than the U.S. state UI systems. Mexico currently does not have an UI system. In the United States, the trade adjustment assistance program provides extended durations of UI benefits to workers whose displacement is certified as being due to trade, and currently requires that these workers undergo training (unless an exemption is granted) as a condition of receiving the extended benefits. While more than 500,000 unemployed workers actually received TAA benefits in 1980, there were only 19,000 recipients in 1990.[14]

To generate widespread political support for continued increased economic integration may require generous programs to partially compensate displaced workers who become unemployed, as are found in many EC nations. However, empirical evidence for the United States, Canada, and the United Kingdom suggests that higher benefit levels and longer durations of eligibility for benefits both lead to longer durations of unemployment.[15] Most studies find no evidence that more generous UI systems ultimately lead unemployed workers to find better jobs.[16] Thus the generous UI systems that may be needed to win political support for continued increased economic integration also have a social cost; namely, the output loss caused by increased durations of unemployment.

As noted in chapter 1, labor mobility is facilitated across states in the United States and across EC nations in Europe by provisions that permit workers to continue to receive benefits if they move to other states or nations in search of improved employment opportunities. To date, however, there have been no studies on whether differences in the generosity of UI benefits across states or nations lead to increased mobility of workers across state or national boundaries. Without such flows, or without evidence that the differential costs across nations to firms of differences in UI benefit generosity influence firms' locational decisions (again see chapter 1), harmonization of benefit generosity across nations does not seem to be a precondition for increased economic integration.

14. U.S. Senate Finance Committee (1992, p. 45).
15. Atkinson and Micklewright (1991). Evidence they cite for other EC countries suggests more modest effects in situations in which the monitoring of job search efforts are stronger.
16. An exception is Ehrenberg and Oaxaca (1976).

There is, however, recent evidence that at least one large multinational firm, Hoover, relocated a plant from France to Scotland because of lower wage *and* nonwage costs (including social insurance costs) in the latter.[17] Nothing in current EC law mandates that the generosity of UI or other social insurance benefits must be equal across nations or must exceed a specified level.

Should the United States require that its trading partners establish some form of UI system? For nations located in other continents, insofar as the costs of UI are not fully shifted onto workers in the form of lower wages, the primary beneficiaries of such a requirement would be workers who become unemployed in the other countries. Insofar as employers' costs are increased, however, employment may fall. With respect to Mexico, a reasonable conjecture is that the establishment and operation of a Mexican UI system might also serve to reduce the incentive of unemployed Mexican workers to become illegal immigrants to the United States, although it might also result in an increase in the number of unemployed Mexicans.

Training and Job Placement Programs

Notice of impending job loss and the provision of unemployment insurance benefits to help moderate earnings loss and provide resources to help finance a job search do not exhaust the range of services that can be provided to displaced workers. All OECD nations also offer some forms of job search assistance, usually through a public employment service that maintains listings of jobs vacancies and job applicants. In some European nations, such as Sweden, the public employment service is the central labor market intermediary in the nation, and all job vacancies are listed with it.[18] In other nations, such as the United States, the employment service competes with many private labor market intermediaries and typically finds itself listing, and helping to fill, primarily lower-level, lower-paying jobs.[19] How regularly unemployed workers must report to the employment service and use its resources in order to maintain eligibility for UI benefits also varies widely across nations.

All OECD nations also have programs that provide training for displaced workers who become unemployed. In some, such as Sweden, all unemployed job seekers who fail to find employment after a series of

17. "The Hoover Affair and Social Dumping" (1993).
18. "Unemployment Benefit Rules and Labour Market Policy" (1991, p. 217).
19. Bishop (1992).

placement and counseling services are placed in retraining centers. Each year about 2 percent of the Swedish labor force is retrained at these centers.[20] In contrast, in other nations, such as the United States, participation in government-supported or subsidized training programs is largely voluntary and at a lower level. An exception to the voluntary programs in the United States is the small-scale trade adjustment assistance program, in which, as noted earlier, to qualify for extended weeks of benefits, a worker displaced for trade-related reasons must enroll in a retraining program or be granted an exemption.

Finally, most, but not all, OECD nations have programs in which the government subsidizes the employment of unemployed workers. The government usually does this by serving as a temporary employer of last resort, by providing selective wage subsidizes to reduce the costs of hiring unemployed workers by private sector firms, or by helping unemployed workers to start up their own new businesses.

Table 5-5 presents comparative data (for 1989, 1990, or 1990–91) on public expenditures on labor market programs, as a percent of gross domestic product, for the three program areas just mentioned and for programs for youth and the disabled. Care must be taken in interpreting these numbers because they depend heavily on government reporting systems, on the extent to which private institutions coexist that perform similar functions, and on the level of unemployment in each economy. Quite strikingly, these percentages vary widely even within the EC nations. For example, Germany spent 0.22 percent of its GDP on public employment service activities, and Italy spent only 0.08. Similarly, Denmark spent 0.65 percent of its GDP on labor market training (for adults), but Spain spent only 0.10 percent, and subsidized employment represented 0.63 percent of Belgium's GDP but only 0.04 percent of France's. Indeed, aggregating expenditures on these three sets of programs, youth measures, and vocational rehabilitation and work for the disabled—measures that are often called active labor market policies by the OECD—expenditures for the EC nations ranged from 1.47 percent (Ireland) to 0.42 percent (Greece) of GDP. Variation among the larger set of OECD nations is even greater, with Australia (0.25 percent), Japan (0.13 percent), and the United States (0.25 percent), all spending a much smaller share of their GDP on these programs than any EC nation does.

Rather than focusing on expenditure shares, one can also measure "effort" by looking at the number of recipients of program services per program employee. Table 5-6, for example, tabulates for various countries the ratios of the number of unemployed persons to two measures of employment by the public employment service. The variation in these

20. Leigh (1992, p. 7).

Table 5-5. *Public Expenditures on Labor Market Programs as a Percent of Gross Domestic Product, Selected OECD Nations, 1989–91*

Country	Year	PES[a] (1)	LMT[b] (2)	YM[c] (3)	SE[d] (4)	DIS[e] (5)	Sum of (1) through (5)
Australia	1990–91	.07	.06	.04	.04	.04	0.25
Austria	1990	.10	.10	.01	.04	.05	0.30
Belgium (EC)	1989	.18	.14	.01	.63	.16	1.12
Canada	1990–91	.21	.27	.02	.02	n.a.	n.a.
Denmark (EC)	1989	.09	.65	.26	.03	.32	1.35
Finland	1990	.10	.25	.05	.42	.12	0.94
France (EC)	1989	.12	.32	.20	.04	.05	0.73
Germany (EC)	1990	.22	.38	.04	.15	.23	1.02
Greece (EC)	1989	.08	.18	.04	.12	.01	0.42
Ireland (EC)	1990	.16	.49	.39	.29	.14	1.47
Italy (EC)	1988	.08	.03	.69	★	★	0.80
Japan	1990–91	.02	.03	★	.10	.01	0.13
Luxembourg (EC)	1990	.03	.02	.12	.06	.13	0.37
Netherlands (EC)	1990	.08	.19	.06	.05	.62	1.04
New Zealand	1989–90	.08	.43	.08	.16	.03	0.78
Norway	1990	.13	.35	.12	.18	.20	0.99
Portugal (EC)	1990	.11	.14	.12	.09	.07	0.52
Spain (EC)	1989	.12	.10	.08	.50	★	0.80
Sweden	1990–91	.21	.47	.05	.13	.72	1.58
Switzerland	1990	.06	.01	★	★	.09	0.17
Turkey	1989	.01	.04	.05	.04	★	0.15
United Kingdom (EC)	1990–91	.14	.22	.18	.02	.03	0.59
United States	1990–91	.08	.09	.03	.01	.04	0.25

Source: *OECD Employment Outlook, July 1991* pp. 237–49.

n.a. Not available.

★Less than .005 percent.

a. Public employment services and administration.

b. Labor and market training for the unemployed and employed.

c. Youth measures (including training and apprenticeship).

d. Subsidized employment (wage subsidies, support of unemployed starting businesses, direct job creation).

e. Vocational rehabilitation and work for the disabled.

ratios across countries is enormous. For the first measure, the ratios vary by a factor of almost 14 across the EC nations; for the second measure they vary by a factor of 10. That is, the United Kingdom has ratios that are one-fourteenth and one-tenth the size of the respective ratios in the EC countries that devote the least resources to the public employment service.

Table 5-6. *Unemployed Persons per Staff Member in Public Employment Services, Selected OECD Nations, 1988*

	Unemployed persons per staff member in	
Country	Employment offices	Employment offices plus network and program management
Australia	109	58
Austria	74	49
Belgium (EC)	n.a.	80
Canada	213	82
Denmark (EC)	81	61
Finland	55	43
France (EC)	271	122
Germany (EC)	86	57
Greece (EC)	n.a.	360
Ireland (EC)	733	251
Netherlands (EC)	152	131
New Zeland	175	120
Norway	68	47
Portugal (EC)	266	120
Spain (EC)	713	n.a.
Sweden	14	10
Switzerland	15	15
Turkey	n.a.	1,380
United Kingdom[a] (EC)	53	36

Source: *OECD Employment Outlook, July 1991*, table 7.7.
n.a. Not available.
a. 1989 data.

The data in tables 5–5 and 5–6 suggest that economic integration does not appear to require harmonization of the levels of active labor market policies across trading partners. It should be intuitive why it does not. The levels of public services demanded depend, among other things, on private labor market institutions, the heterogeneity of the skill composition of the labor force, and the wealth level of a nation—factors that vary widely across nations.

Furthermore, one should not presume that more of a service, such as training, is necessarily good. For example, evidence on the impact of training and employment programs in the United States on the durations of unemployment of unemployed workers and on their post-unemployment earnings is mixed.[21] Moreover, costs must be taken into account as well as benefits. Recent evidence for the United States suggests that the effects of placement services, counseling, and other types of job search assistance are often as effective as, or more effective than, training, and are considerably cheaper.[22] Clearly each nation must choose its own level and mix of services, based on its own needs, resource levels, and evaluation of the relative cost-effectiveness of the different programs.

Although harmonization of policies is not required for increased economic integration, to win political support certain policies may be needed to help finance "adjustment programs" in areas where unemployment is high for trade-related or other reasons. For example, in the United States, federal employment and training program and employment service funds are allocated to each state at least partially according to the number of unemployed workers in the state.

Similarly, the European Social Fund, which provides funding for retraining and resettlement allowances, and the European Regional Development Fund, which funds development initiatives in underdeveloped or declining regions, both concentrate their resources on the EC member nations, and within nations on the regions, that have the greatest needs for such assistance. Funding for these programs, which are operated by the EC itself, come primarily from customs duties levied on imports from nonmember nations, a value-added tax in all member nations, and a tax on each nation equal to a fixed percent of its GDP.[23]

Can this supranational redistributive system persist over time? With the incorporation into the EC of the poorer southern members (Greece, Portugal, and Spain), other EC nations are undoubtedly transferring resources to these countries. Their incorporation into the EC and such transfers make sense only if the gains to the original members of an expanded EC are larger than the subsidies being made to the newer members. Although the gains are hard to estimate, a set of EC nations with growing economies and low unemployment rates will facilitate the belief that integration is worthwhile. In contrast, stagnant EC national economies, with high unemployment rates, will most likely modify that belief and lead to pressure to reduce the subsidies.

21. Manski and Garfinkel (1992).
22. Leigh (1990).
23. Molle (1990, p. 75).

Chapter 6

Who Can Work and How Working Conditions Are Established

THE determination of who can work in a country and the rights workers have to decide upon their work environment are two more aspects of labor markets that are influenced by, and will influence the future extent of, economic integration. The first section in this chapter deals with immigration policies and the types of foreign workers allowed to permanently, or temporarily, seek work in a nation. The next section discusses the determination of whether a worker is qualified to work in an occupation, either by governments or professional associations. The final section examines collective bargaining and whether workers have the right to be formally involved in discussions over their working conditions through employee participation schemes, such as the European Work Councils.

Immigration Policies

This section compares and contrasts immigration policies first in the North American continent and then among the members of the European Community. It discusses how these policies influence, and are influenced by, the extent of economic integration.

The United States, Mexico, and NAFTA

All nations limit the flow of people who may *legally* enter their country to seek permanent or temporary employment. In many nations a key criteria for admission to a country is how the skills of the applicant match the labor market needs of the nation. In the United States, family reunification currently remains the category under which most legal immigrants are admitted. Many nations also have "guest worker" programs in which foreign workers are admitted into a country for a specified period of time to meet temporary labor market needs. An example in the United States is the temporary agricultural worker program, or H-2A program of the 1986 Immigration Reform and Control Act, which permits the import of foreign migrant workers during peak agricultural employment seasons.[1]

An important policy concern in the United States has been the impact of large flows of unskilled legal and illegal immigrants on the earnings of domestic low-skilled workers. Although one might predict that a large increase in the supply of unskilled workers would have an adverse effect on the wages of unskilled workers, to date the available evidence does not suggest that communities which have been the recipients of large immigrant flows have seen the wages of their domestic low-skilled workers decline relative to the wages of comparably skilled workers in other communities.[2]

In part, this finding may reflect the fact that immigrants increase the demand for products, and thus the demand for labor, as well as the supply of labor. In part, it may reflect the fact that a large flow of immigrant labor to a community causes potential domestic migrants to the community to change their destinations or induces some domestic workers who reside in the community to move elsewhere in search of better employment opportunities.[3] That is, the fact that communities which have been recipients of large immigrant flows have not seen their unskilled workers' wages fall relative to those of comparable workers elsewhere may indicate that these immigrant flows also have indirectly caused the wages of unskilled workers to fall in other communities. Indeed, one study concluded that the growth in the United States in unskilled workers between 1975 and 1985, which was due primarily to immigration, was an important reason that the wages of unskilled workers fell substantially relative to the wages of skilled workers nationwide during the period.[4]

Much of the immigration of low-skilled workers into the United States consists of legal and illegal immigration from Mexico. The wage differentials between the two countries are so large (see chapter 4) and the treatment of unemployed workers so different (as noted in chapter 5, there is no unemployment insurance system in Mexico) that such a flow of workers is almost inevitable. To the extent that NAFTA has the

1. Pierce (1993, pp. 35–36).
2. Altonji and Card (1991); Butcher and Card (1991); Card (1990); LaLonde and Topel (1991).
3. Filer (1992).
4. Borjas, Freeman, and Katz (1992).

potential to improve employment opportunities in Mexico, its passage may reduce the flow of Mexican immigrants to the United States, which, other things equal, would put upward pressure on unskilled wages in the United States.[5]

In contrast, moving to a deeper form of economic integration and allowing free mobility of workers between countries, as the EC does, would almost certainly lead to increased migration of Mexican workers to the United States.[6] Mexicans who previously were discouraged from becoming illegal immigrants would no longer have to fear being apprehended when they tried to cross the border, and they would encounter better employment opportunities in the United States because they now could be employed legally "on the books."

Although increased migration of unskilled workers to the United States would lower the earnings or increase the unemployment of domestic workers with whom the immigrants are most substitutable, or do both, the aggregate real income of American citizens would increase as long as immigrants were paid no more than their marginal products *and* as long as immigrants' payroll, income, sales, and property taxes were no less than the services or payments they receive from the government. If these conditions were met, the potential would exist for the domestic "winners" from free migration to compensate the domestic "losers" and still leave everyone at least as well off as they were before the policy change.

Since the losers from increased freedom of migration are likely to be concentrated in geographic areas near Mexico and among lower-skilled workers and since the benefits to the winners are more diffuse and less obvious, political pressure will arise for such compensation to be a precondition for deeper integration. For example, just as organized labor and its supporters in the United States argued that the expansion of income support and retraining programs should be a precondition for the passage of NAFTA, they would probably also argue that the expansion of such programs should be a precondition for the approval of any form of deeper integration that increased the migration of Mexican workers to the United States. Put another way, just as proposals to provide compensation for workers displaced by foreign trade are often part of the political debate when governments seek to win approval of free trade agreements, proposals to provide compensation for workers displaced by immigrants

5. Of course, other things are not equal. NAFTA will also probably decrease the demand for unskilled workers in the United States, which will put downward pressure on their wages.

6. Chapter 16 of NAFTA does in fact provide for increased "temporary entry for business persons." These provisions apply primarily to high-skilled workers and should not increase the flow of low-skilled Mexican workers to the United States. See Ortiz Miranda (1993, pp. 16–19).

would probably be part of the political debate when governments seek to win approval for increased freedom of mobility of workers.

American citizens as a group can lose from increased immigration, which would preclude the possibility of such compensation, if immigrants receive government services (such as schooling) and payments (such as unemployment insurance and welfare), whose costs are greater than the taxes that immigrants pay. Although the available evidence to date suggests that immigrants to the United States have historically "paid for themselves" when it comes to comparing taxes paid and public expenditures received, this evidence has usually applied to people who migrated to the United States before 1980.[7] But even this evidence shows that, on average, more recent cohorts of immigrants use the welfare system more intensively than earlier cohorts did. Moreover, illegal immigrants are not eligible for many social services (such as unemployment insurance and welfare). Converting them to legal immigrant status would immediately boost those costs. Furthermore, as the expansion of Mexican immigration to California, Arizona, and New Mexico has shown, infrastructure needs, such as school construction, can greatly increase. And to the extent that immigrants also tend to be overrepresented in the lower part of the earnings distribution, they may well impose substantial costs on the rest of society.[8]

Even if they do not impose costs, so that unambiguously increased immigration benefits American citizens as a group, the problem remains that the major government expenditures for immigrants, such as the cost of their children's schooling, may be borne at the state and local level. Yet a large share of the governmental revenues that the immigrants provide accrues to the federal government in the form of federal income and social security payroll tax revenues. An expansion of Mexican immigration to the United States would exacerbate this imbalance. Thus, to win approval of deeper economic integration between the United States and Mexico, political considerations may also require programs in which the federal government compensates state and local governments for some of the costs to them of increased immigration.

The European Community

The EC has had the objective of promoting free mobility of labor across member nations ever since its inception.[9] Since July 1968 citizens

---

7. Borjas (1990); Borjas and Trejo (1991).

8. Caution is advised here. For although young adult immigrants *may* impose substantial costs in some areas (such as education), they also may currently be substantial net contributors in other areas (such as social security).

9. An excellent discussion of this topic, from which I freely draw, is found in Flanagan (1993).

of every EC nation have been able to accept employment in any other EC nation on equal terms with residents of that second nation.[10] A series of directives and resolutions, many of which were discussed in previous chapters, provide freedom for citizens of EC member nations to move freely between nations, to maintain residency in other nations after employment, to be employed in other nations, to be eligible for all social insurance programs in other nations on the same terms as citizens of those nations, and for mutual recognition of professional qualifications across member states.[11]

In spite of these efforts, mobility of citizens between member states has been quite low. Table 6-1 contains data from each EC country on the number of its citizens living in each of the other EC member nations for a year in the late 1980s. Row C at the bottom of the table summarizes these data by presenting for each member nation the ratio of the number of EC nationals from other EC countries living in the nation divided by the total labor force of the nation. Even though the numerator includes family members who are not in the labor force, the ratio is 0.05 or less in all EC nations except France and Belgium, where it is 0.07 and 0.13, respectively.[12]

Why has there been such a small movement of workers across national boundaries in the EC? Part of the answer is that the intracountry mobility of workers also tends to be lower in EC nations than it is in the United States. Table 6-2 presents representative data on regional mobility rates for the United States and the four largest EC nations in 1987. The rate for the United States is 50 percent more than the highest EC nation rate. Moreover, empirical evidence suggests that inter-area migration flows within EC nations are much less sensitive to wage and unemployment differences than are interstate migration flows within the United States.[13] Some have attributed this lower intracountry European mobility to the high costs of buying and selling residences in Europe.[14]

Part of the explanation for low EC intercountry mobility rates may also be the language and cultural differences among EC nations. More important, however, may be the fact that real wages historically have

10. Citizens of Spain and Portugal, which were admitted to the EC in 1986, fully received such rights effective January 1, 1993.

11. These include EC Council directives 64/220, 64/221, 68/360, 72/194, 75/34, 75/35, 75/362, 77/452, 78/686, 78/1026, 80/154, 81/1057, 85/384, 85/433, 87/540, 89/48, 90/364, and 90/365, and EC Council regulations 1621/68, 1251/70, 1408/71, and 574/72. For details see European Information Services (1990, pp. 13–72, 133–294, 580–945).

12. Data were not available to make this calculation for Luxembourg.

13. Eichengreen (1993).

14. See Gene Koretz, "Europe's Work Force Isn't Moving with the Money," *Business Week,* June 24, 1993, p. 24.

Table 6-1. *European Community Citizens Living in Another Member State*
Thousands

| Country of citizenship | Living in | | | | | | | | | | | | Citizens living in another EC state as share of home country's 1986 labor force[e] |
	B^a	D^a	G^a	GR^b	S^c	F^a	IR^a	IT^a	L^a	N^a	P^a	U^d	
Belgium	...	*	18	1	10	50	n.a.	4	n.a.	23	1	*	0.025
Denmark	2	...	13	1	5	2	n.a.	1	n.a.	1	*	*	0.009
France	92	2	72	6	24	...	n.a.	17	13	7	3	28	0.001
Germany	24	6	...	11	39	44	n.a.	25	n.a.	39	4	43	0.007
Greece	19	*	275	...	1	8	n.a.	12	n.a.	4	*	13	0.085
Ireland	1	1	8	1	1	2	...	1	n.a.	3	*	532	0.427
Italy	250	2	509	6	13	334	n.a.	...	n.a.	16	1	75	0.051
Luxembourg	5	*	5	*	*	3	n.a.	*	...	*	*	*	0.077
Netherlands	61	2	97	3	14	14	n.a.	4	20	...	2	20	0.040
Portugal	11	*	71	*	31	765	n.a.	2	33	8	...	13	0.211
Spain	50	1	126	1	...	321	n.a.	7	n.a.	18	7	30	0.039
United Kingdom	21	10	83	16	65	34	n.a.	17	n.a.	37	7	...	0.010

(Table continued on next page)

Table 6-1 (*continued*)

Thousands

Addenda	Living in												Citizens living in another EC state as share of home country's 1986 labor force[e]
	B[a]	D[a]	G[a]	GR[b]	S[c]	F[a]	IR[a]	IT[a]	L[a]	N[a]	P[a]	U[d]	
(A) Total other EC residing in nation	537	25	1,276	46	193	1,577	66	90	n.a.	157	25	766	...
(B) 1986 labor force in nation	4,212	2,816	28,024	3,888	14,147	24,009	1,308	23,851	167	5,843	4,481	27,771	...
(C) (A)/(B)	0.13	0.01	0.05	0.01	0.01	0.07	0.05	**	n.a.	0.02	0.01	0.03	...

Sources: For citizens living abroad, Commission of the European Communities (1992b); for the 1986 labor force, *OECD Employment Outlook, September 1988*, table D.

n.a. Not available.

*Fewer than 1,000.

**Less than 0.005.

a. 1988.

b. 1987.

c. 1982.

d. 1985–87.

e. Computation treats missing data for Ireland and Luxembourg as zeros.

Table 6-2. *Percent of Total Population That Changed Region of Residence in 1987, United States and the Four Largest EC Nations*

Country	Percent	Number of regions
France	1.3	22 regions
Germany	1.1	11 Länder
Italy	0.5	a
United Kingdom	1.8	10 regions (excludes Northern Ireland)
United States	2.7	51 states

Source: *OECD Employment Outlook, July 1990*, table 3.3.

a. Not described in the original source.

varied little across the original six member nations, and thus citizens of those countries do perceive the gains from mobility to be sufficiently large to give up family, friends, language, and culture.

Table 6-3, which presents data on indexes of hourly compensation costs for production workers in each EC nation, illustrates this point. The index is set equal to 100 for the United States in each year and then computed for the other countries by taking account of exchange rate differences. In 1975 the index was close to 100 in four of the original six member nations and in the low 70s in France and Italy. Insofar as these indexes are representative of earnings opportunities throughout each country, workers had virtually no incentive to migrate across national boundaries in Belgium, Germany, Luxembourg, and the Netherlands. Apparently the roughly 30 percent compensation cost differentials between France and Italy and the other original EC nations were not high enough to offset the costs of movement, including language and culture.

In 1989 the range of the compensation cost index across the original six EC nations was still roughly 30 points; the index varied from 89 in France to 123 in Germany. However, the compensation cost index in five of the six more recently admitted members varied from 19 in Portugal to 73 in the United Kingdom.[15] The new members clearly increased the dispersion of compensation costs and thus the potential returns to migration across national boundaries in the EC.

Some evidence that hourly cost differentials and other economic forces have influenced migration flows among EC nations is found in the last column of table 6-1. There I have computed an estimate of the total citizens of each EC nation living in other EC nations in the late 1980s as a share of the home nation's 1986 labor force.[16]

15. Denmark, with an index of 107, is similar to the original six EC nations.

16. These computations treat missing data for Ireland and Luxembourg as zeros, and thus the calculations should be viewed as suggestive only.

Table 6-3. *Indexes of Hourly Compensation Costs for Production Workers in EC Nations, 1975, 1989*[a]

Country	1975	1989
Original members		
Belgium	101	115
France	71	89
Germany	100	123
Italy	73	92
Luxembourg	100	97[b]
Netherlands	103	107
1973 members		
Denmark	99	107
Ireland	47	66
United Kingdom	52	73
1980s southern members		
Greece (1981)	. . .	38[b]
Portugal (1986)	. . .	19
Spain (1986)	. . .	64[c]

Source: U.S. Department of Labor (1990b, table 1).

a. Index is set equal to 100 for the United States in each year. Hourly compensation costs measure the costs to employers, not the value to workers. Indexes are adjusted to reflect exchange rate differences.

b. Data are for 1987.

c. Data are for 1988.

The largest ratio, roughly 0.43, is in Ireland, and the bulk of its expatriates are found in the United Kingdom. Although the hourly cost index difference between these two nations is small, only 7 points in 1989, the standardized unemployment rate in Ireland was one of the highest in the EC in the late 1980s (see table 3-8) and thus the economic pressures for migration were high. The United Kingdom is the closest EC nation to Ireland, and, of course the two nations' common language and culture facilitate migration.

The second highest ratio, 0.211, is in Portugal. Portugal was by far the poorest EC nation, as measured by the hourly labor cost index, in 1989 (table 6-3). Even though the EC's freedom of movement provisions did not yet fully apply to Portuguese citizens in the late 1980s, many of them were living in other EC nations, with the vast majority in France. Not surprisingly, the third highest ratio, 0.085, is found in Greece, which was the second poorest EC nation. Except in the small nation of Luxembourg, the ratio was below 0.05 in all the other EC nations.

These results suggest that large differences in standards of living have the potential, even in Europe, to bring about large international migra-

Table 6-4. *Foreign Employees in EC Nations, 1987*

Country	Foreign employees as percent of total employees	Share of EC citizens in total foreign employment (percent)
Belgium	6.2	75.2
Denmark	1.7	29.2
France	6.4	50.3
Germany	6.9	31.1
Greece	1.3	26.5
Ireland	2.5	81.4
Italy	n.a.	n.a.
Luxembourg	37.4	94.7
Netherlands	3.6	49.0
Portugal	1.1	29.9
Spain	n.a.	n.a.
United Kingdom	3.8	48.5

Source: Commission of the European Communities (1992a, table 4).
n.a. Not available.

tion flows. As the EC contemplates expansion to include the still poorer eastern European nations, the flow of migrants is likely to expand and lead to downward pressure on real wages in the more developed nations. Indeed, the migration flow has already started under the label of "political refugees." To stem the flow of migrants from the east will require policies to expand the economies of the eastern European nations. In this sense, the EC members' dilemma is similar to the one the United States faces with respect to Mexico.

Table 6-4 more concisely presents data on foreign employees, as a percent of total employment in each EC nation in 1987 (except Spain and Italy, for which data are not available). Ignoring the data for Luxembourg, which primarily reflects employees of the EC itself, these data suggest that in six of the nine other EC nations for which data are available, other EC nationals make up a minority of foreign employees. Pressures for migration from lower-income nations, whether they be in eastern Europe, Asia, or Africa will continue, almost independent of policies that seek to restrict the entry of such people.

Does increased international migration of workers reduce the incentives of nations that are exporters of highly educated workers to invest in higher education? Put another way, if a brain drain is induced in some countries by increased economic integration, will these "exporting nations" find it less profitable to invest in schooling, which will result in lower levels of education and income in their economies. In general the answer is yes, which has lead some economists to propose placing a tax on highly educated labor that emigrates.[17] However, if an excess supply of skilled labor exists in an economy (due to a downward rigid money wage), emigration can serve to decrease unemployment and raise the earnings of those who remain. Furthermore, to the extent that emigrants send home remittances to help support their friends and family members who remain in the country, the total earnings of those who remain plus the remittances may exceed the nation's pre-emigration level of earnings.[18] Hence increased mobility of highly educated workers will not necessarily cause reductions in schooling investments in countries that export such workers.

Occupational Qualifications

More than 500 occupations have some form of occupational licensing in the United States. These range from occupations that require large investments in postcollege education, including the professions of law, medicine, and dentistry, to occupations that require much less education and training, such as cosmetology.[19] While licensing occasionally occurs at the national level—for example, board certification of physician specialties such as surgery occurs at the national level based on a doctor's training, experience, and performance on a certification exam—licensing normally occurs at the state level and is determined either by a governmental regulatory board or by members of the profession. An example of the latter is the American Bar Association, which, through statewide bar examinations and reciprocity agreements, determines which potential lawyers may practice in each state.

While presumably the goal of occupational licensing is to improve the quality of practitioners in an occupation and thus to guarantee minimum quality standards to consumers, the regulation of entry into an occupation may also serve to limit supply and thus to increase the earnings of incumbent practitioners. Many studies indicate that states with more restrictive occupational licensing requirements in an occupation, other factors held constant, have higher earnings for practitioners in the occupation.[20] A smaller number of studies also show that more restrictive

17. See, for example, Bhagwati and Partington (1976).

18. Such remittances can be important to developing countries. Funkhouser (1992) estimated that they were equivalent to 8.6 percent of El Salvador's gross domestic product in 1987.

19. For general discussions of occupational regulation in the United States, see Rottenberg (1980); Young (1987).

20. See, for example, Kleiner (1990); Kleiner, Gay, and Green (1982); Kleiner (1992) and the references cited therein.

reciprocity agreements limit the flow into a state of experienced practitioners from other states.[21]

Table 6-5 presents information on the average percent of test takers
who passed the 1991 bar examinations in each state, a requirement for
new lawyers who want to practice in the state. It also presents information on the reciprocity arrangements for experienced out-of-state lawyers
who want to practice in each state. The number passing state bar examinations varied from 53 percent in California to 90 percent in Arkansas.
With respect to experienced lawyers, sixteen states had no provisions for
reciprocity and required all experienced attorneys who wanted to practice law in their states to take the bar exam. Six other states required
experienced lawyers to retake a portion of the bar exam or to take a
special test. Seven states effectively had bilateral reciprocity agreements
with other states; the remaining twenty-one states and the District of
Columbia admitted into practice all experienced lawyers who were admitted to the bar (licensed to practice) either in all other states or in all
other states that had passage of the bar examination as a criterion for
admission to practice.

How, within the context of a single nation, can such differences in
occupational licensing requirements persist across states? In the case of
law, practitioners might argue that state laws have evolved in different
directions in different states and thus that competency in one state's law
does not necessarily imply competency in another's. Skeptics might
argue that incumbents in a profession have powerful interests in limiting
supply and that different licensing requirements across states simply
reflect differences in the political power of the profession across states.
Similar arguments can be made to explain why differences in occupational qualifications across nations exist in many occupations.

In Europe, most occupational licensing occurs at the national level.
The founders of the EC understood that to stimulate the flow of semi-
skilled and skilled workers across national boundaries, some actions
either to harmonize occupational qualifications across nations or to
provide for reciprocity of recognition of qualifications were required.

Initially the EC sought to harmonize occupational qualifications among
member nations. Between 1975 and 1985 it passed seven directives
providing for mutual recognition in medical-related professions.[22] But
progress on adopting directives in other professions was slow. For example, although discussions on establishing of standards for architects and

21. See Kleiner, Gay, and Greene (1982); Loucks (1983); Pashigian (1980).
22. These include directives 75/362 (doctors), 77/452 (nurses), 78/686 (dentists),
78/1026 (veterinarians), 80/154 (midwives), 81/1057 (supplemented the previous five
directives), and 85/433 (pharmacists).

Table 6-5. *Average Percent of Test Takers That Passed the State Bar Examinations, and State Reciprocity Arrangements, 1991[a]*

State	Passing percent	Reciprocity arrangement	State	Passing percent	Reciprocity arrangement
Alabama	67	No	Montana	79	Yes, B,P
Alaska	63	Yes, A,P	Nebraska	76	Yes, A or P
Arizona	73	No	Nevada	75	No
Arkansas	90	No	New Hampshire	68	No
California	53	No, S	New Jersey	65	No
Colorado	75	Yes, A,O	New Mexico	81	No
Connecticut	71	Yes, B,P	New York	61	Yes, R,P
Delaware	60	No	North Carolina	72	Yes, R,P
District of Columbia	55	Yes, A,P	North Dakota	83	Yes, B,P
Florida	73	No	Ohio	80	Yes, B,P
Georgia	72	No, S	Oklahoma	86	Yes, B,P,E
Hawaii	64	No	Oregon	74	No
Idaho	86	No, S	Pennsylvania	77	Yes, R,P
Illinois	83	Yes, R,P	Rhode Island	80	No, S
Indiana	85	Yes, B,P	South Carolina	83	No
Iowa	72	Yes, B,P	South Dakota	80	No
Kansas	87	No	Tennessee	66	Yes, A,P
Kentucky	84	Yes, A,P	Texas	74	Yes, B,P
Louisiana	59	No	Utah	88	No, S
Maine	72	No, S	Vermont	76	Yes, B,P
Maryland	69	Yes, A,P,S	Virginia	74	Yes, R,P
Massachusetts	71	Yes, A,P,S	Washington	76	No
Michigan	74	Yes, B,S	West Virginia	75	Yes, R,P
Minnesota	71	Yes, B,S	Wisconsin	83	Yes, R
Mississippi	80	No, P,S	Wyoming	74	Yes, B,P
Missouri	86	Yes, B,P			

Source: Author's interpretation of material found in *BAR/BRI Digest* (Washington: BAR/BRI, 1993).

a. If a state held more than one bar examination in a year, an unweighted average is used.

A. All states that require passage of an exmaination.

B. All states.

E. An examination is required if the state requires an examination for Oklahoma applicants.

O. Years of practice or passage of the bar examination in another state is required.

P. Years of practice requirement.

R. Only for states that have reciprocity with the state.

S. Practicing attorneys who meet years of practice requirements only need to take part of the bar examination or a special attorney's examination.

engineers began in 1968, the first directives harmonizing standards for architects were not adopted until 1985, and standards for engineers have yet to be adopted.[23]

As a result, the EC shifted gears and in 1989 passed directive 89/48, which deals with mutual recognition of qualifications for occupations that require at least three years of higher education. However, when the length of period of study, or the content of study, differs across nations, the directive allows for the administration of examinations to judge the qualifications of applicants from other EC nations or for a requirement that applicants work under the supervision of a licensed professional in the country for a specified time before the applicants' occupational qualifications are certified.[24] Such provisions obviously serve to limit the mobility of professionals across EC national boundaries.

Collective Bargaining and Worker Participation

In the mid-1950 approximately 33 percent of nonagricultural employees in the United States were union members.[25] This percentage fell steadily over the next forty years, and by 1992 membership in unions and employee associations (organizations such as the National Educational Association, whose concerns historically related to professional standards but are increasingly involved in collective bargaining) had fallen to 16 percent of nonagricultural employment.[26] Many factors are believed to be responsible for the decline in unionism in the United States, including the changing demographic structure of the work force, the changing industrial mix of employment, the changing regional distribution of employment, increased foreign competition in manufacturing, the deregulation of a number of industries, and increased employer resistance to unions.[27]

The decline in unionization in the United States began before the increased economic integration of the United States with the world economy, and several of the factors mentioned do not depend on increased economic integration. Nonetheless, growing economic integration is clearly partially responsible for the continuation of the trend, in that the manufacturing industries hit most heavily by foreign competition

23. Holmstedt (1991, pp. 101–03).
24. European Information Services (1990, pp. 279–93).
25. Space constraints limit my discussion here of collective bargaining and worker participation. For excellent treatments of how economic integration has influenced these two issues in Europe, see Reder and Ulman (1993); Turner (1993); Streece (1993).
26. Ehrenberg and Smith (1994, table 13.1).
27. See, for example, Farber (1987); Farber and Krueger (1992).

Table 6-6. *Bargaining Structure and Union Membership in EC Nations*
Percent

Country	Level of negotiation, 1990	Union density[a]		
		1970	1980	1988
Belgium	Sectoral	46.0	56.5	53.0
Denmark	Sectoral	60.0	76.5	73.2
France	Regional, plant, sectoral	22.3	19.0	12.0
Germany	Sectoral	33.0	37.0	33.8
Greece[b]	National central, sectoral	. . .	35.8	25.0
Ireland	National central	. . .	68.1	78.3
Italy	Sectoral	36.3	49.3	39.6
Luxembourg[b]	Sectoral	46.8	52.2	49.7
Netherlands	Sectoral, company	37.0	35.3	25.0
Portugal[b]	Sectoral, plant	59.0	58.8	30.0
Spain[b]	Sectoral, regional, plant	. . .	22.0	16.0
United Kingdom	Sectoral, company, plant	44.8	50.7	41.5

Sources: For level of negotiation, European Trade Union Institute (1991, table VIII); for union density, *OECD Employment Outlook, July 1991*, table 4.1.

a. Percent of employees who are union menmbers. The data often are for an adjacent year.

b. Union membership includes all recorded (not necessarily employed) members.

were among the most heavily unionized in the United States. Foreign competition has led both to a decline in domestic employment in these industries and to a shift, within the domestic industries, from unionized to nonunionized employment. Incentives for the latter came from the large wage differentials that existed in the United States between unionized and nonunionized workers of comparable quality, differentials that some estimate ranged from 20 to 25 percent in the 1980s.[28]

Is a decline in union membership a necessary result of increased economic integration? Table 6-6 presents data on the percent of employees that were union members in each of the EC nations in 1970, 1980, and 1988. Definitions of union membership vary widely across nations— some countries, for example, include unemployed union members in their total—so these data should not be used to make intercountry comparisons.[29] They can, however, be used to trace how the extent of unionization has varied in individual nations over time.

28. Blanchflower and Freeman (1992).

29. See "Trends in Trade Union Membership" (1991, pp. 98–100). It is instructive to note how different some of these OECD union membership data are from the union coverage data obtained from other sources reported in Blanchflower and Freeman (1992,

In Belgium, Denmark, Germany, Italy, Luxembourg, and the United Kingdom, union density rose during the 1970s but then fell back somewhat during the 1980s. Union density rose during the 1980s in Ireland but fell in Greece and Portugal. It fell throughout the period in France, the Netherlands, and Portugal. Undoubtedly, the decline during the 1980s in union density in most EC nations reflected the prolonged high unemployment rates of the 1980s, which hit the heavily unionized manufacturing sectors hardest.

Will such declines in density continue? A goal of the EC is to stimulate employment growth by widening each nation's market, and *if* this goal is accomplished aggregate employment may be expected to eventually increase.

Will the increased employment be among unionized or nonunionized employees? Bargaining in the EC nations is often done at the national or sectoral level, and in some countries, such as Germany, sectoral agreements can be extended to nonunion employers at the discretion of the government (table 6-6). As a result, union-nonunion wage differentials are often much lower in the EC nations than they are in the United States, and thus the incentive to shift production to nonunion sites is also lower.[30] Insofar as employee benefits in the EC come primarily through social insurance programs that apply to all employers rather than through privately negotiated benefits, the EC nations also have less incentive to seek nonunion production sites to avoid employee benefit costs than the United States has. Hence future employment growth in the EC nations could prove to be unionized employment, and union density may even increase.

To say that union employment may increase is not to say, however, that the structure of collective bargaining will remain constant in the EC nations. Increased international competition and trade (both among EC nations and with other countries), the growth of small firms in the service sector, and the increased diversity of work forces due to the growth of female employment, all create pressures to move away from the centralized or sectoral bargaining that is typical in many EC nations (table 6-6) and toward more decentralized bargaining.[31] The latter, in turn, by making wages less uniform, may lead to more union-nonunion competition and a further decline in union density.

table 1). In part, the difference reflects the fact that workers who are not union members are often covered by union contracts negotiated at the national or sectoral level in some European countries. Thus, in these countries, a decline in union membership is not always associated with a decline in coverage by a union contract.

30. Blanchflower and Freeman (1992, table 3).

31. Streeck (1993); Katz (1993); Hartog and Theeuwes (1993).

Table 6-7. *Workers' Rights to Information, Consultation, and*
Participation in Management in EC Nations, 1991

Country	Systems of works councils[a]	Employee representation[a]
Belgium	Mandated by legislation (100)	. . .
Denmark	Established through collective agreement (35)	On supervisory board (35)
France	Mandated by legislation (50)	On board of directors (50)
Germany	Mandated by legislation (5)	On supervisory board (500)
Greece	Mandated by legislation (50)	On board of certain public or quasi-public enterprises
Ireland	Established through collective agreement[b]	On board of certain public or quasi-public enterprises
Italy	Established through collective agreement	On board of certain public or quasi-public enterprises
Luxembourg	Mandated by legislation (150)	On board of directors (1,000)
Netherlands	Mandated by legislation (35)	5
Portugal	Mandated by legislation	. . .
Spain	Mandated by legislation (50)	. . .
United Kingdom	Established through collective agreement[b]	. . .

Source: Commission of the European Communities (1992c, pp. 101–06).

a. The numbers in parentheses are minimum number of employees for establishment to be covered.

b. Rarely occurs.

A decentralization of collective bargaining, coupled with a decline in union density, would most likely diminish the ability of unions to influence working conditions at individual firms. As such, unions in EC nations have been forcefully pushing for the expansion of employee information, consultation, and participation in management decision rights, as a way to increase, or at least protect, employee control over their work environments.

Table 6-7 summarizes the rights workers in EC nations already had as of 1991. Eight EC nations mandate employee participation in the form of systems of work councils (although small employers are often exempted). These vary across countries in terms of whether they include management as well as worker members, the rights of the work councils to information on economic, financial, and social matters, their rights to be consulted on decisions, their ability to negotiate issues, and their rights to share in decisionmaking. Denmark, Italy, Ireland, and the United Kingdom establish such councils under collective bargaining agreements, but only rarely do work councils actually occur in the latter two countries. About half of the EC nations also have statutory or collectively bargained provisions, again with small employers often exempted, that provide for employees to have representatives on boards of directors or on supervisory boards.[32]

The EC's Maastricht Social Charter, agreed to in 1989 by all member nations except the United Kingdom, calls for an expansion of employee information, consultation, and participation rights.[33] Not surprisingly, unions push for mandating such rights while management opposes them, except when they perceive that increases in productivity will result from employee participation.[34] Managers resist increased mandates for worker participation because they want to retain as much flexibility as possible in the face of increased international competition. The relative political weakness of EC unions makes the short-run prospects for increased mandated worker participation quite poor.[35]

32. The distinction is that boards of directors have final responsibility for the day-to-day running of a business, whereas supervisory boards appoint (and fire) the management team that runs a business day-to-day.

33. Addison and Siebert (1991, table 1).

34. Levine and Tyson (1990) survey the literature on the productivity effects of worker participation schemes.

35. Turner (1993).

Chapter 7

Looking to the Future

*L*ABOR markets and labor market institutions affect the prospects for increased economic integration. Increased economic integration also affects labor markets and labor market institutions. In this concluding chapter, I look to the future and address a set of issues that relate to these two statements.

I begin by discussing perhaps the best example of economic integration that exists, the integration of the fifty state economies in the United States. Certain lessons can be drawn from the U.S. experience and usefully applied to international economic integration. The discussion suggests that increased economic integration does *not* require a harmonization of labor market standards, of real social insurance levels, or of occupational qualifications across nations.

I then examine whether greater integration necessarily even increases efficiency in the labor market and consider the efficiency-equity trade-off inherent in greater economic integration. The latter issue suggests that some expansion in social protection and convergence of labor market standards across nations may be required if continued increased economic integration is to be *politically* feasible among nations at vastly different stages of development.

Legislation mandating social protection or labor market standards in themselves are meaningless unless they are enforced. I turn in the last section to a discussion of noncompliance with existing legislation and the options that exist to try to ensure compliance with new bilateral or multilateral agreements. The costs of higher standards and of ensuring compliance with them may, in fact, be too high for nations at lesser stages of development to bear. Richer nations directly, or indirectly may therefore have to bear some of those costs if they demand that higher standards or improved compliance be a precondition for increased economic integration. I conclude that the vast differences in standards of living and real wages between developed and developing countries, which provide much of the potential gain from economic integration, are also a source of opposition to greater integration and may serve to limit its future growth.

Lessons from the U.S. Experience

The integration of the fifty state economies goes back to the U.S. Constitution, which prohibits states from imposing taxes to restrict the flow of goods and services across state borders.[1] As the U.S. economy evolved, a system of protective labor legislation and social insurance emerged that involves shared federal and state responsibility.

The federal social security system (discussed in chapter 3) is a single national system that provides a base level of retirement income, disability insurance, and medical insurance for the aged. The base level of retirement income that individuals receive is determined by their lifetime earnings and is not tied to their specific employers. Thus the system facilitates mobility of employees across employers and states.[2]

Many other social insurance programs in the United States, however, are not federal programs, but rather are programs under the control of the individual states. Examples are unemployment insurance (see chapters 1 and 5), aid to families with dependent children (AFDC), and workers' compensation. Although the federal government shares in the funding of some of these programs—for example, it finances additional weeks of benefits for unemployed workers who have exhausted their regular UI benefits in high-unemployment states—the states determine the weekly benefit levels under each program.

In fact, these benefit levels vary widely across states. For example, in January 1993 the AFDC benefit level for a family of four ranged from $144 a month in Mississippi to $1,025 a month in Alaska, a range far greater than can be explained by cost-of-living differences.[3] Similarly, in the same month the maximum weekly unemployment insurance benefit level varied from $154 in Nebraska and South Dakota to $468 in Massachusetts.[4] This variation again far exceeded cost-of-living differences across states.

1. Constitution of the United States of America, Article 1.
2. As discussed in chapter 3, employer-based retirement plans in the United States often limit labor mobility.
3. U.S. House of Representatives Ways and Means Committee (1993, table 12).
4. National Foundation for Unemployment Compensation and Workers' Compensation (1993, table 18).

How can individual states have such different real benefit levels? Some evidence (cited in chapter 1) shows that differences in at least AFDC benefit levels influence interstate migration levels, and to the extent that UI payroll taxes are not fully shifted onto workers, employers in high real UI benefit level states will have, other things equal, higher costs of doing business. That real benefit levels have *not* converged across states over time suggests both that states differ in their willingness to provide social insurance benefits to workers and that high-benefit states are willing to "pay the price" (higher payroll taxes, higher business costs, and thus higher prices for their products) of having higher benefit levels to achieve what they consider equitable treatment of workers.

The implication of these differences is that economic integration at the international level does *not* require a harmonization of *real* social insurance levels. Nations that place greater weight than others on providing insurance against risks of unemployment, work injuries, or financial need can do so if they are willing to pay the price.

What about labor market standards? A uniform federal minimum wage implies a great variation in the value of the minimum wage relative to prevailing wages across states (see chapter 4). Moreover, states also vary in the extent that state minimum wage laws cover workers not covered by the federal minimum wage law. Some states also have state minimum wages that exceed the federal minimum wage. The implication here is that international economic integration does *not* require a harmonization of labor market standards and that some nations may voluntarily choose to have higher standards than others.

How can differences in social insurance levels, labor market standards and, for that matter, real wages persist over time? There is evidence that real wages have been converging across states in recent decades in the United States.[5] More important, however, growth rates of employment have differed across states, with low real wage states growing more rapidly than high real wage states.[6] Although to some degree differential growth rates reflect immigration patterns, they largely reflect domestic interstate migration.[7] That is, labor market adjustments in the United States have primarily taken the form of population movements rather than the rapid convergence of wages, benefit levels, and standards across states.

The flow of population to growing low real wage states has helped to prevent persistent unemployment rate differences between states. Evidence from European countries suggests, however, that interarea migra-

5. See Barro and Sala-i-Martin (1991); Blanchard and Katz (1992).
6. Blanchard and Katz (1992).
7. See Crandall (1993, pp. 1–24).

tion flows within European nations are much less sensitive to wage and unemployment differences than interstate flows are in the United States.[8] It is therefore unlikely that intercountry European labor mobility among the EC nations will rise to U.S. interstate levels by the elimination of barriers to intercountry mobility in those nations. Hence demand shocks that affect EC nations differentially may lead to persistent unemployment rate differences among EC countries.

When states in the United States experience temporarily high unemployment rates and find their economies depressed, the federal government takes actions to redistribute income to the states that are hardest hit.[9] This redistribution occurs automatically both through declining income tax payments to the federal government in the depressed states and through the formulas used to allocate employment service, employment and training program, and extended unemployment insurance benefits, all of which contain a component based on area unemployment rates.

Both these automatic stabilizers and active labor market policies (see chapter 5) help to reduce the amount of interstate labor market migration that occurs in response to temporary changes in economic conditions. Such migration, which otherwise might make sense to workers, at least in the short run, would exacerbate a region's economic problems and would lead to increased social costs.[10]

Presumably, to protect countries from temporary fluctuations in demand that economic integration exacerbates, a supranational redistributive body will also be necessary. Attempts by the EC to institute such a body have been only partly successful because the entire budget of the EC is less than 2 percent of the member nations' total gross domestic product.[11] Whether nations will cede more of their output to a supranational redistributive body is an open question.[12]

Finally, in the United States occupational standards are typically determined at the state level by state agencies or professional association members, or both. The reciprocity agreements described in chapter 6 for experienced lawyers who want to practice law in other states include a mixture of implicit bilateral agreements ("we will admit anyone who admits our residents"), bilateral agreements that require extra training

8. Eichengreen (1993).

9. Sala-i-Martin and Sachs (1991) show that in the United States declining federal taxes and increasing federal transfers offset about one-third of regional-specific declines in income.

10. See Bluestone and Harrison (1982).

11. Eichengreen (1992).

12. The interrelationship between economic integration and redistributive issues is the subject of a forthcoming Brookings book by Susan Collins in this series.

("we will admit anyone who admits our residents and who can pass an examination on our state-specific laws"), and outright prohibitions ("we will treat experienced lawyers from out of state like any newly trained applicant to the bar"). Even though such a system may be less efficient than a system of certification at the national level and does serve to restrict mobility, its persistence suggests that the harmonization of occupational qualifications that the EC is seeking to establish is not required for economic integration. Rather, a system of implicit bilateral agreements, such as operates for lawyers in the United States, is a feasible option.

Efficiency, Equity, and Political Considerations

As discussed in chapter 1, many people support increased economic integration of the world economy because of its potential to enhance economic efficiency. Increased trade is thought to do so by allowing nations to specialize in the production of those goods for which they have a comparative advantage and by allowing them to take advantage of any economies of scale in production that may result from having a larger market for their goods. Increased capital and labor mobility is thought to allow capital-labor ratios to equalize across nations and thus to bring about the equality of marginal productivities of capital and of labor across nations, which in turn should maximize total world output.[13]

However, increased economic integration also leads to increased competition in the output market, and that in turn is likely to lead to reduced job security for workers and increased voluntary and involuntary labor mobility within a nation. As discussed in chapter 3, increased mobility may lead to a reduction in economic efficiency for two reasons. First, reductions in workers' expected job tenure diminish both employers' and employees' incentives to invest in firm-specific training, and lower levels of training in turn lead to lower levels of productivity. Second, reductions in expected job tenure limit employers' ability to strategically use the shape of life-cycle compensation profiles to stimulate all employees to exert more effort. To date, how much these kinds of efficiency losses may at least partially offset the potential gains from increased economic integration has not entered the policy debate.

13. Many other efficiency-enhancing possibilities permitted by increased economic integration exist. These include reductions in transaction costs if a common currency is available, increased productivity due to competition-induced reductions in x-inefficiency, and enhanced rates of technology transfer. Many of these are discussed more fully in other volumes in this series.

Increased economic integration also results in a host of distributional issues. Much of the benefit from increased integration accrues to society as a whole in the form of lower prices for consumers. However, the losses may fall most heavily on people from certain geographic areas or demographic groups. For example, the industries affected most heavily by increased foreign competition are concentrated in a few geographic areas.[14] To take another example, in the debate over NAFTA, many expressed widespread concern about the probable impact NAFTA would have on American manufacturing workers.[15]

Insofar as there are "identifiable" losers from increased economic integration, the political process will most likely lead to demands for expanded domestic adjustment policies, such as retraining programs or income support programs, to ensure political support for increased integration and to reduce changes in the distribution of income that are considered undesirable. As noted in earlier chapters, income support and social insurance programs are less generous in the United States than they are in most EC nations. Similarly, the level of resources that government devotes to training and retraining is much lower in the United States than in most EC nations (table 5-6).

NAFTA was passed over the vehement objections of the American labor movement and without a substantial enhancement of any training or income support program. But the enhancement issue will no doubt be constantly raised in the political debate as a precondition for support for continued increased economic integration. Whether such enhancement will occur is uncertain; many people argue (but there is little hard evidence) that the failure of European nations to generate more jobs during the 1980s and early 1990s was due in part to the generosity of their programs.[16] Indeed, in December 1993 the EC Commission itself proposed lowering employer contributions to social insurance programs in member nations as a way to stimulate employment growth.[17]

If an aim of increased economic integration is to permit increased mobility of workers across national borders as EC policies have striven to achieve, one must be aware that increased international migration of workers may also systematically influence the distribution of earnings of the native workers in a country. For that reason, as discussed in chapter 6, the political process will also lead to proposals for income support or retraining programs to assist workers displaced by foreign migration as

14. For evidence for the United States, see Shelburne and Bednarzik (1993).

15. See, for example, Lustig, Bosworth, and Lawrence (1992).

16. Blank and Freeman (forthcoming).

17. Roger Cohen, "European Community Backs Plan to Create Jobs by Reducing Costs," *New York Times*, December 10, 1993, p. A6.

a precondition for support for freer mobility of labor, just as policies to aid workers displaced by foreign trade normally enter into the policy debate over free trade.

American citizens as a group can lose from increased immigration if immigrants receive government services and transfer payments in excess of the taxes they pay. Even if that does not happen, the major governmental expenditures society makes on behalf of immigrants (for example, the costs of their children's schooling) are borne at the state and local levels, whereas much of the revenue that immigrants provide to government accrues to the federal government (for example, income taxes). To the extent that increased immigration is concentrated in certain regions of the country, political considerations also suggest that to facilitate integration that provides for freer mobility of labor, programs may have to be established in which the federal government compensates state and local governments for some of the costs to them of increased immigration.[18]

Finally, deeper economic integration is inevitably linked with employment standards. As discussed in chapter 4, almost all nations establish employment standards, or minimal conditions under which they believe people should be employed. Examples are minimum wage and maximum hours laws, child labor and compulsory schooling laws, occupational safety and health laws, equal employment or antidiscrimination laws, and laws governing the conditions under which workers can be dismissed.

As noted in chapter 4, critics of free trade argue that it is both an immoral decision and unfair competition for the United States to make a free trade agreement with a nation that either has much lower employment standards than we do or fails to enforce its existing standards. In the early debate over NAFTA, opponents argued, and the Clinton administration agreed, that the treaty should not be signed unless a side agreement was established to guarantee Mexico's adherence to standards in the areas, among others, of minimum wages, child labor law, and occupational safety and health. When the Clinton administration negotiated such an agreement, the debate shifted to whether the side agreement was comprehensive enough and sufficiently guaranteed compliance.

Pressure for requiring potential trading partners to improve both their labor market standards and their employers' compliance with these standards as a precondition for increased economic integration stems from at least two concerns. First is concern for the well-being of children and

18. Indeed, by mid-1994, California had filed suits against the federal government in an effort to recoup the costs to the state of providing health and educational services to *illegal* immigrants and their dependents, as well as the costs of jailing felons who are *illegal* immigrants. Similar suits had also been filed by Arizona and Florida.

other low-skilled workers in potential trading partners; second is concern for domestic workers who may lose their jobs because of what some perceive as unfair competition if unregulated free trade is permitted. By requiring potential competitors to improve their standards before granting them free trade status, a nation increases their costs, reduces their comparative advantage, and thus reduces domestic job loss, as well as, unfortunately, the gains from trade.

The first concern is surely a legitimate one. Requiring trading partners to adhere to some minimum level of morality in their behavior should be a precondition for free trade. For example, under existing U.S. law, the United States does not permit the import of goods produced using slave or coerced prison labor.[19] The problem is how to determine what appropriate minimum standards should be for nations that are at much lower levels of development than the United States, how to ensure compliance with these standards, and how to decide what full or partial kinds of exemptions to permit. These are difficult tasks without simple answers. Moreover, setting minimum standards that are too generous or requiring nations to devote too many resources to compliance will reduce those nations' comparative advantage and exports, reduce their employment growth, and thus hurt the very people that in principle one wants to help.[20]

If the first concern is really the motivation for pressing for improved standards and compliance in potential trading partners, the United States should take care to require standards that do not serve merely to increase the costs and thus eliminate the jobs of the very citizens of its trading partners who supporters of improved foreign standards and compliance allege they are trying to help. The United States might also consider mechanisms that allow the Americans who benefit from free trade to partially bear the costs of improved standards or compliance abroad. That might be done if the United States partially pays for the costs by remitting back to the trading partner funds raised through general tax revenue or through a tax on the traded goods.

The second concern is less likely to be a legitimate one. Raising a competitor's costs through tariffs or through requiring it to expend resources to ensure compliance with improved standards reduces its comparative advantage and thus the gains *both* countries can achieve from trade. It is far better to compensate the people hurt by free trade for their losses and to provide adjustment assistance to minimize those

19. See, for example, U.S. Senate Finance Committee (1986); U.S. House of Representatives Foreign Affairs Committee (1992).

20. The role that developing nations will play in an increasingly integrated world economy is the subject of a forthcoming book by Anne Krueger in this series.

losses. Insofar as free trade does yield benefits to the United States as a whole, resources can in principle be made available for these purposes.

Ultimately the political process may lead to improved standards and compliance abroad as a precondition for free trade even if the sole true motivation for them is the second one. However, as apparently happened with occupational safety and health standards in the EC nations, the benefits that accrue to workers of U.S. trading partners from these changes may come primarily from the real income growth that free trade permits, not from the mandated improved standards themselves.

Indeed, as real wages have risen in a nation, historically workers have used some of these real wage increases to "purchase" improved working conditions. That is, as productivity and real wages have increased, workers have borne some of the employers' costs of improving working conditions, by accepting smaller real wage increases. Thus the real income growth that free trade permits in lesser developed U.S. trading partners may have a much greater impact on working conditions in those nations than any standards the United States tries to mandate that they impose.

Compliance

Although the failure of Mexican employers to comply with their nation's existing labor standards was a major issue in the debate over NAFTA, the extent to which American employers do or do not comply with U.S. labor laws was rarely mentioned. As discussed in chapter 4, studies suggest that in the United States there is significant noncompliance with labor standards, including minimum wage, overtime hours, child labor, and occupational safety and health legislation.

Noncompliance regarding employer contributions to social insurance programs also seems to exist in the United States. A recent study of a representative sample of employers found that 45 percent underreported at least some of their employees' taxable wages to state unemployment insurance systems.[21] Underreporting of taxable wages, and hence underpayment of unemployment insurance payroll taxes, was a more serious problem for small firms than for large; the former underreported 14 percent of their total payroll and the latter underreported 4 percent.

The main source of underreporting was the erroneous classification of employees, who are covered by the unemployment insurance system, as independent contractors, who are not covered by the system. Because employers are also not required to make contributions for independent

---

21. Blakemore and others (1993).

contractors to the federal social security and state workers' compensation systems, the implication of this study is that significant noncompliance may also be present in both those programs. The authors also found that noncompliance rates were higher in firms that faced higher unemployment insurance payroll tax rates. This finding suggests that increasing the generosity, and hence the cost, of social insurance programs provides employers with greater incentives for noncompliance.

Noncompliance is also present in the United States with respect to the labor laws that govern collective bargaining, and the extent of noncompliance appears to have increased over the last thirty years.[22] Noncompliance in the labor standards, social insurance, and labor law areas occurs in the United States because the resources devoted to monitoring and enforcing compliance are low, as are the penalties, at least for first-time offenders (see chapter 4).

Surprisingly, the issue of noncompliance with labor standards and social insurance laws has not recently received as much attention in Europe.[23] One study did find, however, that considerable noncompliance existed among Spanish employers in regard to their contributions to the Spanish social security system, which provides health care, sick leave, and retirement benefits to workers.[24] Noncompliance was concentrated in the small establishment, "underground sector," of the Spanish economy. Spanish employers face no criminal charges if convicted of underpayment and only have to pay back payroll taxes owed plus a 20 percent penalty. Given high rates of unemployment in Spain, noncompliance is apparently tolerated by both the government and unions because they fear that rigorously enforcing the law would put many small employers out of business and create large job loss.

These studies imply that to ensure compliance with labor standards, social insurance laws, and collective bargaining laws, governments must invest substantial resources in monitoring and enforcing compliance or must establish heavy penalties for employers convicted of noncompliance. That this has not been done in the United States suggests that apparently the benefits it perceives from increased compliance do not exceed the resource costs (including potential job loss) to which such actions would lead. The studies also suggest that the levels at which standards are set, or the generosity of social insurance programs, are inversely related to compliance rates.

22. Flanagan (1989).
23. It did receive considerable attention during the late 1970s and early 1980s in discussions of the size of the informal sector or underground economy. See, for example, Tanzi (1982).
24. De La Rica and Lemieux (forthcoming).

If compliance with existing national laws, or with standards mandated by a supranational body (for example, EC directives), is a precondition for agreement to increased economic integration, how can nations ensure that their trading partners will comply? As described in the appendix to chapter 1, the EC relies on a combination of the EC Commission, national courts, and the Court of Justice, to monitor and ensure compliance. The Commission and the Court can conduct investigations of individual firms and impose fines if they judge that a violation has occurred. But ultimately such judgments must be enforced by the member states.[25]

It is likely to be a time consuming process for the Commission to investigate individual employers, and the Commission's and the Court's lack of enforcement power means that the process will probably not prove effective in the long run. If ultimate enforcement lies in the hands of the member states, should not the responsibility for monitoring and ensuring compliance also lie there?

The labor side agreement to NAFTA takes this approach.[26] Responsibility for monitoring and enforcing a nation's labor legislation rests on that nation. Any complaint by individuals or another nation that the nation has failed to enforce its own laws goes to the nation's chief labor official (in the United States the secretary of labor). Representatives of the three nations would then try to negotiate a settlement. If they cannot agree and the complaint asserts that the failure is both *persistent* and has had an effect on trade, a panel of experts would be convened. If the panel ruled against the country, the country would have sixty days to develop an enforcement plan satisfactory to the complaining party. If no settlement was reached within the time limit, fines of up to $20 million dollars could be imposed on the country, and if the country still refused to comply, the other countries could raise tariffs or cancel other trade concessions.

Can such a system succeed? In part it will depend on how *persistent* is defined. For example, will the 10 to 25 percent noncompliance rates observed in the United States for minimum wage and overtime pay legislation be judged to be persistent? One possible outcome is that the side agreement will force the United States to devote more resources to enforcing compliance in its own country and that the principal effect of the system will therefore be to increase compliance in the United States.

25. Many of the cases brought before the Court by the Commission relate to whether a statute in a member state conforms to an EC directive. If the judgment is that it does not, the member state is the one to enforce the judgment (that is, change its own law).

26. Anthony De Palma, "Law Protects Mexican Workers but Its Enforcement Is Often Lax," *New York Times*, August 15, 1993, pp. 1, 14; "How Complaints Would Be Handled," *New York Times*, August 14, 1993, p. A45.

In part, the success of the system will depend on whether countries will be permitted to revise their labor laws to provide exemptions for small establishments in which either it is extremely costly to monitor and enforce compliance or the costs to employers of compliance will create substantial job losses. In part, it will depend on whether nations will be permitted to decrease, as well as increase, the stringency of their standards or the generosity of their social insurance schemes. Nothing in the labor side agreement specifies the level at which each nation must set its standards or programs.[27]

Ultimately, however, one must return to a point made earlier. Less-developed nations, like Mexico, may not now have the resources to set their labor standards or the generosity of their social insurance programs at levels that the political process in developed nations may require if widespread support for economic integration is to be generated in the developed nations. Similarly, they may not now have sufficient resources to ensure compliance with even their existing standards or programs.

NAFTA was passed without the United States' negotiating any increases in Mexico's labor standards, in large part because President Clinton succeeded in tying its passage to his ability to conduct future foreign policy and because he made some "political payoffs." However, the process that led to the passage of NAFTA may be the exception rather than the rule. To facilitate greater economic integration with other less-developed nations, the political process in developed nations may require giving the less-developed nations transitional subsidies to help them raise their standards and increase their compliance with those standards to levels that generate widespread support for increased integration in the developed nations. Such subsidies reduce the short-run benefits to the more developed nations from increased economic integration and may be difficult to achieve politically.[28] Thus the vast differences in standards of living and real wages between developed and developing countries which provide much of the potential gain from increased economic integration, may also serve to limit its future growth.

27. In December 1993, for the first time in a number of years, Mexico raised its minimum wages relative to the rate of price inflation it was experiencing. Anthony DePalma, "Mexico Raises Minimum Wages as Pledged," *New York Times,* December 12, 1993, p. A12. At the same time, however, the EC Commission was suggesting to its member states that they reduce their own minimum wages, in an effort to stimulate employment growth. Roger Cohen, "European Community Backs Plan to Create Jobs by Reducing Costs," *New York Times,* December 11, 1993.

28. Susan Collins argues in her forthcoming book that the major economic gains from NAFTA will accrue to Mexico rather than to the United States. In such a situation, it is politically more difficult to ask the developed nation to provide the subsidy.

Comments

Stephen Nickell

Ronald Ehrenberg has presented a magisterial survey of the issues and has included a vast amount of empirical material. He is to be congratulated on producing such a stimulating and comprehensive book. I focus here on a few specific questions in order to complement his work.

In this context, further economic integration means freer trade or increased labor and capital mobility, or both. Generally there are gains to this process, but there are usually some losers who could, in principle, be compensated. Barriers to economic integration will typically be higher the more losers there are or the more significant the losers are in the political process.

If trade is opened up between two "equals," losers are concentrated in those sectors in each country that have a comparative disadvantage. With "unequals"—that is, a rich country and a poor country—the same holds true, but because the losers in the rich country would tend to be among the low-skill workers, a significant increase in inequality could occur. If the rich and poor countries are taken together, however, the result may be a decrease in inequality.

Where do differences in the labor market come in? They are of two basic kinds. The first comprises differences in tastes, technology, human capital, and the stock of knowledge, which lead to differences in real wages and hours of work. With increased integration between rich and poor countries, the real wage differential may well be the *dominant feature*. But it may not be the focus of debate, since little can be done

Stephen Nickell is director of the Institute of Economics and Statistics at Oxford University.

about it. For example, in the now notorious case (in Britain and France) of the transfer of some production by Hoover Ltd. from France to Scotland, noted in chapter 5, the fact that payroll taxes are lower in Scotland is cited as an important reason for the move. But since wages are considerably lower in Scotland than in France, this factor was probably important, too.

The second set of labor market differences are those caused by governments in the form of laws, regulations, taxes, and so on. Do these create really important barriers to increased economic integration and must they be removed or greatly modified? On balance, Ehrenberg's answer to this question is no, and I would agree. However, on occasion, these labor market features do cause integration to create more losers and may therefore have some effect on the process of integration at the margin. To analyze this further, I begin by focusing on two key issues: tax incidence and effective labor supply.

Tax Incidence and Effective Labor Supply

Many labor market policies are financed by taxation and have some consequences for labor supply. Unemployment benefits are a classic example. In this section I separate out these two effects, concentrating first on the labor market consequences of pure tax changes.

Tax Incidence and the Labor Market

Consider a standard labor market in an open economy, where W is the nominal labor costs per employee to the firm, P is the price of (value-added) output received by the firm, t_1 is the payroll tax rate, t_2 is the income tax rate, and t_3 is the excise tax rate. Then the demand for labour depends on W/P. If P_c is the consumer price index, the supply of labor depends on the real consumption wage, $W(1 - t_1)(1 - t_2)/P_c$. If P_m is the price of imports, the consumer price index, P_c, is given by

$$P_c = [(1 - s)P + sP_m](1 + t_3),$$

where s is the share of imports. If the tax rates are small, the real consumption wage can be written as vW/P, where the wedge, v is given by

$$v = \left[\frac{1 - (t_1 + t_2 + t_3)}{1 - s} \right] \Big/ \left[1 + \frac{s}{1 - s} P_m / P \right].$$

This analysis immediately indicates that as long as all taxes are strictly proportional, it does not matter whether they are applied to employers, employees, or goods. Their impact on the labor market is just the same.[1] That fact is most important because a casual reading of the literature often gives the impression that payroll taxes are particularly bad for the operation of the labor market and that if they were replaced by a value-added tax, for example, everything would be much better. Furthermore, this analysis shows that an adverse shift in the terms of trade, leading to a rise in the real price of imports, has exactly the same kind of impact on the labor market as does a rise in payroll taxes.

What about incidence? In a standard competitive model of the labor market, an increase in the tax wedge, v, will tend to raise labor costs and lower employment, thereby reducing the competitiveness of firms in the trade sector. However, long-run labor supply elasticities tend to be very low,[2] so that the impact on both labor costs and employment will be very small, with most of the tax increase being borne by the workers. How relevant is this result? Many would argue that it is of little consequence because, in many of the world's labor markets, wages are not determined competitively. Suppose, therefore, that wages are determined noncompetitively, through union bargaining, say, or some efficiency wage mechanism.

In union bargaining, wage rates result from a bargain between firms, whose profits depend on employment and real labor costs, and unions, whose objective depends on employment and real consumption wages. In a typical Nash bargaining model, the union's contribution to the Nash objective takes the form $(vW/P - vA/P)N$, and the firm's contribution takes the form $\Pi(N, W/P)$, where N is employment, A is the pre-tax alternative earnings available to the workers (taxed at the same rate as earnings inside the firm), and Π is the firm's profit. Then the standard Nash objective is

$$[(vW/P - vA/P)N]^\beta [\Pi(N, W/P)]^{1-\beta}.$$

In this case, whether or not bargaining takes place over employment, the wage outcome is independent of the tax wedge, v.

A similar result applies in many standard efficiency wage models. For example, in both the effort model and the turnover model, the relevant behavior (effort input or quitting) depends on the ratio of wages in the firm to alternative earnings, which is independent of the tax wedge, v. Of course, in some circumstances this neutrality result will not apply, nota-

1. Of course, various detailed characteristics of the tax system, such as progressive income taxation and limits to the coverage of excise taxes, will invalidate this simple result. It nevertheless represents a simple baseline null hypothesis from which to start.

2. The impact is very small and negative for men, somewhat larger and positive for (married) women, and very close to zero, on average.

bly when unemployment benefits are untaxed,[3] or in the case of the Nash bargaining model, when individual utility is not isoelastic.[4] Also, if there is a barrier below which wages cannot fall, because of minimum wages, for example, that will automatically nullify the neutrality result. More important, this is a long-run result, and in many circumstances one might envisage the tax wedge as influencing wages in the short run but not in the long run. For instance, any tendency for individual well-being to be influenced by changes in, as well as levels of, real income will have this effect. In the end, however, the issue is empirical. So what does the evidence tell us?

In a comprehensive attack on the question by James Symons and Donald Robertson,[5] reported in the 1990 *OECD Employment Outlook* and referred to by Ehrenberg, the conclusion is that, in the long run, rises in the tax wedge are borne entirely by labor. However, on average for sixteen OECD countries, a 1 percent rise in the tax wedge induces an immediate rise in labor costs of ½ percent, and nearly half this effect remains after five years. In other words, short-run effects are both significant and long lasting. It is therefore no surprise that time-series analysis on individual countries sometimes detects permanent tax effects, simply because discriminating between these and very long lasting temporary effects is tricky. Thus Anthonie Knoester and Nico van der Windt find permanent tax effects in ten OECD countries, and some labor taxes appear to have permanent effects in Nordic countries and Italy.[6] In my view, however, significant *permanent* tax wedge effects on labor costs do not seem plausible unless there is a fixed floor to wages.

Effective Labor Supply

Many labor market policies not only involve changes in taxation but also *influence* the effective labor supply. Thus, for example, increases in the generosity of the unemployment benefit system reduce the effective labor supply, whereas improvements in maternity benefits or health insurance tend, on balance, to increase it. What are the implications of a change in

3. Expected alternative earnings can be written as $(1 - \varphi)\overline{W}v + \varphi Bv$, where B is unemployment benefit, $\overline{W}$ is the alternative wage, and ϕ is the proportion of the relevant period spent unemployed. If benefits are not taxed, post-tax alternative earnings are $\overline{W}v[(1 - \varphi) + \varphi B/v\overline{W}]$, and a rise in taxation is equivalent to a rise in the benefit replacement ratio.

4. The Nash objective in the text assumes risk neutrality on the part of union workers. If they are risk averse, the union contribution is $\{[U(vW/P) - U(vA/P)]N\}^{\beta}$. So long as U is isoelastic, v only enters multiplicatively and hence will not influence the wage outcome.

5. *OECD Employment Outlook, July 1990*, annex 6.

6. Knoester and van der Windt (1987); (for Nordic countries) Calmfors (1990); (for Italy) Padoa-Schioppa (1990).

effective labor supply? Typically, a fall in effective labor supply will tend to raise wages and reduce employment, which implies a contraction of both imports and exports as well as of economic activity in general. But the main loss after a reduction in effective labor supply comes from the overall fall in economic activity. The purely trade effects are of secondary significance.

To summarize, therefore, *in the long run,* the trade effects of tax-funded changes in labor market benefits are not likely to be important. Over the short to medium term, however, tax effects can generate significant changes in labor costs. So an increase in payroll taxes, for example, will lead to a rise in labor costs, resulting in a reduction in competitiveness and finally, under floating exchange rates, a depreciation of the domestic currency. That could be the end of the story, with the impact of the payroll tax being offset by the rise in prices. But in fact the currency depreciation also leads to a rise in import prices and thus to an additional rise in the wedge, v, putting *further* upward pressure on labor costs. In other words, if payroll taxes are not shifted onto labor in the short run, neither are adverse shifts in the terms of trade. This implies that payroll taxes can, in the short run, influence both trade and employment patterns and that these effects will not normally be undone by exchange rate movements.

The Labor Market and Barriers to Integration

In this section, I look at some specific issues and see how they might relate to increases in integration.

HOURS OF WORK. As Ehrenberg notes in chapter 2, there are wide variations in annual working hours across countries. He sees no reason why this should serve as a barrier to integration or that hours will converge as integration proceeds. Some countries do have regulations on annual hours, but many exceptions exist, noncompliance is common, and moonlighting enables individuals to make their own adjustments. It may, however, turn out that capital mobility will encourage firms that want their employees to work long hours, because of high set-up costs, for example,[7] to locate in unregulated countries.

BENEFITS OF ALL TYPES. Ehrenberg has collected a large body of information on all types of benefit systems, and clearly enormous variations exist both in the extent of the benefits and in the methods of funding. I do not see these variations as being a significant barrier to

7. In many deep-mined coal sites, for instance, it takes up to one hour to reach the coal face from the surface.

integration, essentially because I believe that in the long run the taxes are borne by labor and the benefits per se do not have much effect on a country's trading position. The argument that having low benefits and hence low payroll taxes represents "unfair" competition is wrong.

HEALTH AND SAFETY, MINIMUM WAGES, CHILD LABOR. Variations in these kinds of regulation are more of a barrier to integration than universal taxes and benefits because their impact can be localized in specific sectors. For example, the cost of implementing health and safety regulations could, in some sectors, far outweigh the benefits perceived by individual workers. Under these circumstances, a significant part of the costs in these sectors would be borne by the firms, and that might be enough to put the latter at a disadvantage relative to foreign firms in the same sector. Firms in this sector would then lobby strongly either against free trade or in favor of the same regulations being applied to foreign firms.

Variations in minimum wage laws or child labor laws can easily disadvantage low-skill worker groups in the country where workers are better protected, thereby generating another significant lobby against integration. It could, however, be argued that this lobby is an easy one to ignore and hence does not serve as a significant barrier.

EMPLOYMENT PROTECTION LAWS. Although some of the overall costs of employment protection legislation may be borne by labor in the form of lower wages, this fact will not offset the behavioral impact of these laws. Thus firms faced by strong employment protection legislation will suffer from a loss of flexibility and will find it more expensive to cope with variations in demand. As a consequence, even if the average costs of the legislation are borne by labor, firms that operate in "high-variance" industries will lose out relative to their competitors in countries without employment protection.

Conclusion

A close reading of Ehrenberg's excellent and informative book leads one to conclude that benefit systems and labor market regulations do not serve as a powerful barrier to the extension of economic integration, nor need they be systematically harmonized. Even though labor market differences can lead to changes in the pattern of gainers and losers from increased integration, the number of losers is not significantly increased by these differences.

Richard B. Freeman

Will economic integration eliminate differences in labor practices across countries? I put this question that motivates Ron Ehrenberg's book more sharply that he has done. It is an important question, with implications for economic outcomes and labor institutions and policy.

On the wage and employment side, the question is one of factor price equalization[1] and (with institutionally determined wages) of the employment of less-skilled workers in developed countries. Is increased economic integration, particularly between developed countries, such as the United States, and less-developed countries, going to reduce the employment and earnings opportunities of low-skilled workers and redistribute income in favor of the more skilled in the advanced countries? Concern over the effects of the North American Free Trade Agreement on jobs made this a heated political issue in the United States in 1993. Given that American low-skilled workers have suffered losses in real earnings for decades, are they headed toward third world wages?

On the institution side, the question is one of preserving national differences. Does increased economic integration, particularly among developed countries, mean that all countries must adopt the same institutional structures and labor standards? Many policymakers and analysts worry that this will occur. The United Kingdom opted out of the social charter to avoid continental labor practices. Germany and France worry about "social dumping" (competitive advantages accruing to countries that have low standards for health, pensions, and so forth) from lower income EC countries and the United Kingdom, as well as from the new market economies of eastern Europe.

Ehrenberg's primary concern is with the institutional differences among developed countries, and in particular with differences that cause differences in labor costs. He discusses the problem of integrating third world economies with those of advanced countries, particularly Mexico with the United States, but does not address the big issue of whether factor price equalization will push the wages of the low skilled in advanced countries toward third world wages. This topic requires a consideration of trade theory and evidence that goes beyond the material in the book. Without necessarily agreeing or disagreeing with Ehrenberg's comments on the issue, I focus on integration among developed countries.

Richard B. Freeman is professor of economics at Harvard University, director of the Labor Studies program at the National Bureau of Economic Research, and executive director of the Comparative Labour Market Institutions program at the Centre for Economic Performance in the London School of Economics.

1. Samuelson (1948).

Here Ehrenberg provides a valuable overview of the characteristics of labor markets in advanced OECD countries. He documents the basic fact that labor conditions, rules, and modes of compensation vary substantially among these successful economies. Employees in different advanced countries "work under different rules." Americans, in particular, work with much less regulation and protection than Europeans do. The share of labor cost that goes to vacations, payroll taxes, and so on is higher in most European countries than in the United States.

Do these differences lead to differences in labor costs? If so, who bears the cost?

Transforming different work rules into costs is a difficult business. It is neither conceptually nor empirically clear that higher labor standards mean higher labor costs. According to the Coase theorem, a rule that alters the property rights to employment between workers and employers may redistribute income without affecting its level. Some rules may reduce costs or raise productivity: health and safety regulations that save lives, for instance, or regulations that establish work councils.[2] There are moral hazard and selectivity reasons for mandating some labor rules. Some rules may also increase costs or lower productivity. The same rule may add to efficiency in one setting but not in another, or have a big effect, positive or negative, in one setting but not in another. We do not have great knowledge of how the practices that Ehrenberg documents fit or do not fit together in coherent labor relations systems.

Ehrenberg stresses two important aspects of the cost issue: the extent to which costs nominally placed on employers are shifted back to workers, and the enforceability of standards. On the shifting issue, he notes that any mandated change in benefits and costs will shift both the supply of labor and the demand for labor. He uses unemployment insurance as his example, but it may be more useful to consider the issue of employment mandates of health insurance that have exercised the country in 1994. An increase in the cost of labor due to mandated employer-purchased health insurance shifts the demand for labor down, which at existing wages would cut employment, as critics of employer mandates note. But if the provision of mandated employer health insurance makes work more attractive, it will also increase the supply of labor, so that the long-term cost will fall partly on workers as well as on employers. Alternatively, if the supply of labor is fixed to the economy, such costs are fully shifted to workers.

The evidence on the shifting of payroll taxes or of employer-mandated benefits is not overwhelming. Ehrenberg concludes that with fixed exchange rates, mandated costs or taxes can affect labor costs and the

2. Freeman and Lazear (forthcoming).

competitive position of enterprises, but goes on to assert that "workers pay for at least a good share of their benefits in the form of lower wages." Since much of the cost of mandated benefits is likely to fall on workers, he concludes that harmonization of policies in various areas ought not to be a precondition for increased economic integration, and conversely that increased integration will not require convergence of such benefits. I believe this is a correct assessment.

There is another route by which economies can adjust to different standards: through changes in exchange rates. If Canadians want to spend more on occupational health and safety standards than Americans, and if the cost of such is not shifted back to Canadian workers, Canadian firms will be at a competitive disadvantage at a particular exchange rate. But then the Canadian dollar will depreciate versus the U.S. dollar, and all Canadians will bear the cost of the higher health and safety standards through the higher cost of imported goods from the United States. Ehrenberg downplays this mode of adjustment because he sees integration as a single market with a currency union, as in the fifty U.S. states. I stress this mode of adjustment because I see integration as reductions in trade barriers in a world with different national currencies and flexible exchange rates.

On enforcement, to the extent that employers or workers skirt rules and standards, they avoid the cost (as well as benefits). I expect that governments, labor, and management evade the most costly regulations—those that have substantial inefficiency losses—and enforce the least costly or most beneficial rules. Spain has a high payroll tax that funds national heath insurance, but also an extensive gray market economy in which firms do not pay this tax. The workers in these firms are usually secondary earners in families whose primary earner's employer pays the tax, giving health insurance coverage to the entire family.[3] With high unemployment, neither the Spanish government nor workers have an incentive to catch the gray market firms.

No one has estimated which of the diverse employment standards and regulations in advanced countries have inefficiency costs, which redistribute property rights at the workplace without cost, and which raise productivity, nor the extent or efficiency of evasion. Extant evidence does suggest, however, that devotees of labor market deregulation often exaggerate the costs of social insurance and labor regulations in their desire to convince governments and the public to reduce or eliminate labor standards and protection. Empirical analyses do not turn up big efficiency losses from most programs.[4] If my "efficient lax enforcement" hypothesis

3. De La Rica and Lemieux (forthcoming).
4. See Blank (forthcoming).

is correct, even programs that would on the face of it have sizable efficiency costs may in fact have only slight adverse effects, along with their redistributive or social benefits.

In sum, I believe that the basic theme of the book—that economic integration will not force all developed countries to harmonize labor practices and standards—is correct. Some differences in labor practices and standards have no effect on labor costs. Some costly differences are shifted back to workers. Other costly differences are shifted to the entire population through currency devaluation. Economic integration will not turn us all into clones of the least common denominator country. *Viva las* differences.

References

Abowd, John M., and Michael Bognanno. Forthcoming. "International Differences in Executive and Managerial Compensation." In *Differences and Changes in Wage Structures*, edited by Richard B. Freeman and Lawrence F. Katz. University of Chicago Press.

Addison, John T., and Pedro Portugal. 1992. "Advance Notice and Unemployment: New Evidence from the 1988 Displaced Worker Survey." *Industrial and Labor Relations Review* 45 (July): 645–64.

Addison, John T., and W. Stanley Siebert. 1991. "The Social Charter of the European Community: Evolution and Controversies." *Industrial and Labor Relations Review* 44 (July): 597–625.

Altonji, Joseph, and David Card. 1991. "The Effects of Immigration on the Labor Market Outcomes of Less-Skilled Natives." In *Immigration, Trade, and the Labor Market*, edited by John M. Abowd and Richard B. Freeman, 201–34. University of Chicago Press.

Angrist, Joshua D., and Alan B. Krueger. 1991. "Does Compulsory School Attendance Affect Schooling and Earnings?" *Quarterly Journal of Economics* 106 (November): 979–1014.

Ashenfelter, Orley, and Robert S. Smith. 1979. "Compliance with the Minimum Wage Law." *Journal of Political Economy* 87 (April): 333–50.

Atkinson, Anthony B., and John Micklewright. 1991. "Unemployment Compensation and Labor Market Transitions: A Critical Review." *Journal of Economic Literature* 29 (December): 1679–1727.

Barnow, Burt S., and Ronald G. Ehrenberg. 1979. "The Costs of Defined Benefit Pension Plans and Firm Adjustments." *Quarterly Journal of Economics* 94 (November): 523–40.

Barro, Robert J., and Xavier Sala-i-Martin. 1991. "Convergence across States and Regions." *Brookings Papers on Economic Activity* 1: 107–58.

Bazen, Stephen, and John Martin. 1991. "The Impact of the Minimum Wage on Earnings and Employment in France." *OECD Economic Studies* 16 (Spring): 199–221.

Becker, Gary. 1975. *Human Capital,* 2d ed. New York: National Bureau of Economic Research.

Beller, Daniel J., and Helen H. Lawrence. 1992. "Trends in Private Pension Plan Coverage." In *Trends in Pensions, 1992,* edited by John Turner and Daniel J. Beller, 59–60. U.S. Department of Labor, Pension and Welfare Benefits Administration.

Bhagwati, Jagdish N., and Martin Partington, eds. 1976. *Taxing the Brain Drain I: A Proposal.* Amsterdam: North Holland.

Bishop, John. 1992. "Improving Job-Worker Matching in the U.S. Labor Market." Working Paper 92–40. Cornell University, Center for Advanced Human Resource Studies.

Blakemore, Arthur, and others. 1993. "An Analysis of Employer Tax Evasion in the Unemployment Insurance Program." Arizona State University, Department of Economics.

Blanchard, Olivier J., and Lawrence F. Katz. 1992. "Regional Evolutions." *Brookings Papers on Economic Activity* 1: 1–61.

Blanchflower, David G., and Richard B. Freeman. 1992. "Unionism in the United States and Other Advanced OECD Countries." *Industrial Relations* 31 (Winter): 56–79.

Blank, Rebecca M., ed. Forthcoming. *Social Protection versus Economic Flexibility: Is There a Trade-off?* University of Chicago Press.

Blank, Rebecca, and Richard B. Freeman. Forthcoming. "Cross National Evidence on the Connection between Social Protection and Economic Flexibility." In Blank (forthcoming).

Bloom, David E., and Adi Brender. 1993. "Labor and the Emerging World Economy." Working Paper 4266. Cambridge, Mass.: National Bureau of Economic Research (January).

Bluestone, Barry, and Bennett Harrison. 1982. *The Disindustrialization of America: Plant Closings, Community Abandonment, and the Dismantling of Private Industry.* Basic Books.

Borjas, George H. 1990. *Friends or Strangers: The Impact of Immigrants on the U.S. Economy.* Basic Books.

Borjas, George H., Richard B. Freeman, and Lawrence F. Katz. 1992. "On the Labor Market Effects of Immigration and Trade." In *Immigration and the Work Force: Economic Consequences for the United States and Source Areas,* edited by George H. Borjas and Richard B. Freeman, 213–44. University of Chicago Press.

Borjas, George H., and Stephen J. Trejo. 1991. "Immigrant Participation in the Welfare System." *Industrial and Labor Relations Review* 44 (January): 195–211.

Butcher, Kristin F., and David Card. 1991. "Immigration and Wages: Evidence from the 1980s." *American Economic Review* 81 (May, *Papers and Proceedings, 1990*): 292–96.

Calmfors, Lars, ed. 1990. *Wage Formation and Macroeconomic Policy in Nordic Countries.* Oxford University Press.

Card, David. 1990. "The Impact of the Mariel Boatlift on the Miami Labor Market." *Industrial and Labor Relations Review* 43 (January): 245–57.

———. 1992a. "Do Minimum Wages Reduce Employment? A Case of California, 1987–89." *Industrial and Labor Relations Review* 46 (October): 38–54.

———. 1992b. "Using Regional Variation in Wages to Measure the Effects of the Federal Minimum Wage." *Industrial and Labor Relations Review* 46 (October): 22–37.

Castillo-Freeman, Alida, and Richard B. Freeman. 1991. "Minimum Wages in Puerto Rico: Textbook Case of a Wage Floor." In *Proceedings of the Forty-Third Annual Meeting of the Industrial Relations Research Association,* edited by John Burton, 243–54. Madison, Wisconsin.

———. 1992. "When the Minimum Wage Really Bites." In *Immigration and the Work Force: Economic Consequences for the United States and Source Areas,* edited by George Borjas and Richard B. Freeman, 177–212. University of Chicago Press.

Commission of the European Communities. 1992a. *Migration and Mobility in the European Community: SYSTEM Papers, 5.* Brussels.

———. 1992b. *A People's Europe.* Luxembourg. April.

———. 1992c. *Social Europe: The Regulation of Working Conditions in the Member States of the European Community.* Vol. 1, supplement 4/92. Luxembourg.

Comparative Tables of the Social Security Schemes in the Member States of the European Communities. 1989. 15th ed. Luxembourg: Office of Official Publications of the European Communities.

Cooper, Philip F., and Alan C. Monheit. Forthcoming. "Does Employment-Related Health Insurance Inhibit Job Mobility?" *Inquiry.*

Cox, James C., and Ronald L. Oaxaca. 1981. "The Determinants of Minimum Wage Levels and Coverage in State Minimum Wage Laws." In *The Economics of Legal Minimum Wages,* edited by Simon Rottenberg, 403–28. Washington: American Enterprise Institute.

Crandall, Robert W. 1993. *Manufacturing on the Move.* Brookings.

"Daily, Weekly and Yearly Rest and Weekly Hours." 1991. *European Industrial Relations Review* 210 (July): 24–26.

De La Rica, Sara, and Thomas Lemieux. Forthcoming. "Does Public Health Insurance Reduce Labor Market Flexibility or Encourage the Underground Economy? Evidence from Spain and the U.S." In Blank (forthcoming).

Disney, Richard, and Erika M. Szyszczak. 1984. "Protective Labor Legislation and Part-Time Employment in Great Britain." *British Journal of Industrial Relations* 22 (March): 78–100.

Ehrenberg, Ronald G., and George H. Jakubson. 1988. *Advance Notice Provisions in Plant Closing Legislation.* Kalamazoo, Mich.: W.E. Upjohn Institute for Employment Research.

———. 1990. "Why WARN? Plant Closing Legislation." *Regulation* 13 (Summer): 39–46.

Ehrenberg, Ronald G., and Ronald Oaxaca. 1976. "Unemployment Insurance, Duration of Unemployment, and Subsequent Wage Gain." *American Economic Review* 66 (December): 754–66.

Ehrenberg, Ronald G., Pamela Rosenberg, and Jeanne Li. 1988. "Part-Time Employment in the United States." In *Employment, Unemployment and Labor Utilization*, edited by Robert A. Hart, 256–81. Boston: Unwin Hyman.

Ehrenberg, Ronald G., and Paul L. Schumann. 1982. "Compliance with the Overtime Pay Provisions of the Fair Labor Standards Act." *Journal of Law and Economics* 25 (April): 159–81.

———. 1982. *Longer Hours or More Jobs? An Investigation of Amending Hours Legislation to Create Employment.* Ithaca, N.Y.: ILR Press.

Ehrenberg, Ronald G., and Robert S. Smith. 1994. *Modern Labor Economics: Theory and Public Policy,* 5th ed. HarperCollins, 1994.

Eichengreen, Barry. 1992. "Comments and Discussion." *Brookings Papers on Economic Activity* 1: 65–70.

———. 1993. "Labor Markets and European Monetary Unification." In *Policy Issues in the Operation of Currency Unions,* edited by Paul Masson and Mark Taylor, 130–62. Cambridge University Press.

European Information Services. 1990. *Compendium of EC Employment and Social Security Law.* London: Buttersworth.

European Trade Union Institute. 1991. *Collective Bargaining in Western Europe in 1990 and Prospects for 1991.* Brussels (June).

Eurostat Labour Force Sample Survey: Methods and Definitions. 1985. Luxembourg: Office of Official Publications of the European Communities.

Eurostat Labour Force Survey: Results 1991. 1993. Luxembourg: Statistical Office of the European Communities.

Eurostat Rapid Reports: Population and Social Conditions 1991.6. 1991. Luxembourg: Statistical Office of the European Communities.

Family and Medical Leave Act of 1993: Law and Explanation. 1993. Chicago: Commerce Clearing House.

Farber, Henry S. 1987. "The Recent Decline of Unionization in the United States." *Science* 238 (November): 915–20.

Farber, Henry S., and Alan B. Krueger. 1992. "Union Membership in the United States: The Decline Continues." Working Paper 306. Princeton University, Industrial Relations Section (August).

Filer, Randall K. 1992. "The Effect of Immigrant Arrivals on Migratory Patterns of Native Workers." In *Immigration and the Work Force: Economic Consequences for the United States and Source Areas,* edited by George H. Borjas and Richard B. Freeman, 245–70. University of Chicago Press.

Flanagan, Robert J. 1989. "Compliance and Enforcement Decisions under the National Labor Relations Act." *Journal of Labor Economics* 7 (July): 257–80.

———. 1993. "European Wage Equalization since the Treaty of Rome." In *Labor in an Integrated Europe,* edited by Lloyd Ulman, Barry Eichengreen, and William T. Dickens, 167–87. Brookings.

Flynn, Patrice. 1992. *Employment-Based Health Insurance: Coverage under COBRA Continuation Rules.* Washington: Urban Institute.

Freeman, Richard, and Edward Lazear. Forthcoming. "An Economic Analysis of Works Councils." In *Employee Participation and Works Councils,* edited by Joel

Rogers and Wolfgang Streeck. University of Chicago Press for the National Bureau of Economic Research.

Funkhouser, Edward. 1992. "Mass Emigration Remittances, and Economic Adjustment: The Case of El Salvador in the 1980s." In *Immigration and the Work Force: Economic Consequences for the United States and Source Areas,* edited by George H. Borjas and Richard B. Freeman, 135–76. University of Chicago Press.

Gruber, Jonathan. 1992a. "The Effect of Group-Specific Mandated Benefits: Evidence from Health Insurance Benefits for Maternity." Working Paper 4157. Cambridge, Mass.: National Bureau of Economic Research (September).

———. 1992b. "State Mandated Benefits and Employer Provided Health Insurance." Working Paper 4239. Cambridge, Mass.: National Bureau of Economic Research (December).

Gruber, Jonathan, and Brigitte Madrian. 1993. "Limited Insurance Portability and Job Mobility: The Effects of Public Policy on Job-Lock." MIT Economics Department.

Gustman, Alan L., Olivia S. Mitchell, and Thomas L. Steinmeier. 1993. "The Role of Pensions in the Labor Market." Working Paper 4295. Cambridge, Mass.: National Bureau of Economic Research (May).

Hamermesh, Daniel S. 1993. *Labor Demand.* Princeton University Press.

———. Forthcoming. "Unemployment Insurance: Goals, Structure, Economic Impacts and Potential Applicability to Developing Economies." In *Labor Market Policies for Managing the Social Cost of Economic Adjustments,* edited by Arvil Van Adams, Elizabeth King, and Zafiris Tzannatos. Washington: World Bank.

Hart, Robert. 1987. *Working Time and Employment.* Boston: Allen and Unwin.

———. 1988. *Trends in Non-Wage Labour Costs and Their Effects on Employment.* Luxembourg: Office for Official Publications of the European Communities.

Hartog, Joop, and Jules Theeuwes, eds. 1993. *Labour Market Contracts and Institutions: A Cross-National Approach.* Amsterdam: North Holland.

Holmstedt, Margareta. 1991. *Employment Policy.* London: Routledge.

Holtz-Eakin, Douglas. 1992. "Health Insurance Provision and Labor Market Efficiency in the United States and Germany." Occasional Paper 158. Syracuse University, Maxwell School of Citizenship and Public Affairs, Metropolitan Studies Program (December).

"The Hoover Affair and Social Dumping." 1993. *European Industrial Relations Review* 230 (March): 14–23.

Industrial Relations Services. 1989. *Termination of Contract in Europe: Dismissal and Redundancy in 15 European Countries.* European Industrial Relations Review (EIRR) Report. London: Eclipse Publications. October.

———. 1990. *Non-Standard Forms of Employment in Europe.* EIRR Report. London: Eclipse Publications. July.

International Labour Office. 1991. "Child Labour: Law and Practice." *Conditions of Work Digest* 10(1): annex 1.

———. 1992. *1992 Year Book of Labour Statistics.* Geneva: International Labour Organization.

Jacobson, Louis, Robert J. LaLonde, and Daniel G. Sullivan. 1993. "Earnings Losses of Displaced Workers." *American Economic Review* 83 (September): 685–709.

Katz, Harry C. 1993. "The Decentralization of Collective Bargaining: A Literature Review and Comparative Analysis." *Industrial and Labor Relations Review* 47 (October): 3–23.

Katz, Lawrence F., and Alan B. Krueger. 1992. "The Effect of the Minimum Wage on the Fast-Food Industry." *Industrial and Labor Relations Review* 46 (October): 6–21.

Kleiner, Morris H. 1990. "Are There Economic Rents for More Restrictive Occupational Licensing Practices?" *Proceedings of the Forty-Second Annual Meeting of the Industrial Relations Research Association.* Madison, Wisconsin.

———. 1992. "Do Tougher Licensing Provisions Limit Occupational Entry? The Case of Dentistry." Working Paper 3984. Cambridge, Mass.: National Bureau of Economic Research.

Kleiner, Morris H., Robert S. Gay, and Karen Green. 1982. "Barriers to Labor Migration: The Case of Occupational Licensing." *Industrial Relations* 21 (Fall): 384–91.

Knoester, Anthonie, and Nico van der Windt. 1987. "Real Wages and Taxation in Ten OECD Countries." *Oxford Bulletin of Economics and Statistics* 49(February): 151–69.

LaLonde, Robert J., and Robert H. Topel. 1991. "Labor Market Adjustments to Increased Immigration." In *Immigration, Trade, and the Labor Market,* edited by John M. Abowd and Richard B. Freeman, 167–200. University of Chicago Press.

Lazear, Edward. 1979. "Why Is There Mandatory Retirement?" *Journal of Political Economy* 87 (December): 1261–84.

———. 1990. "Job Security Provisions and Employment." *Quarterly Journal of Economics* 105 (August): 699–726.

Leigh, Duane E. 1990. *Does Training Work for Displaced Workers: A Survey of Existing Evidence.* Kalamazoo, Mich.: W.E. Upjohn Institute for Employment Research.

———. 1992. "Retraining Displaced Workers: What Can Developing Countries Learn from the OECD Nations?" Working Paper 946. Washington: World Bank, Population and Human Resources Development (August).

Levine, Daniel I., and Laura D'Andrea Tyson. 1990. "Participation, Productivity, and the Firm's Environment." In *Paying for Productivity: A Look at the Evidence,* edited by Alan S. Blinder, 183–236. Brookings.

Loucks, Christine Ann. 1983. "The Effects of Occupational Licensing on Interstate Labor Migration." Ph.D. dissertation. Washington State University.

Lustig, Nora, Barry P. Bosworth, and Robert Z. Lawrence, eds. 1992. *North American Free Trade: Assessing the Impact.* Brookings.

"Maastricht and Social Policy—Part One." 1993. *European Industrial Relations Review* 237 (October): 14–20.

Madrian, Brigitte. 1992. "Employment Based Health Insurance and Job Mobility: Is There Evidence of Job Lock?" MIT Economics Department.

Manski, Charles, and Irwin Garfinkel, eds. 1992. *Evaluating Welfare and Training Programs.* Harvard University Press.

"Minimum Pay in 18 Countries." 1992. *European Industrial Relations Review* 225 (October): 14–21.

Mitchell, Daniel J. B., and Jacques Rojot. 1993. "Employee Benefits in the Single Market." In *Labor in an Integrated Europe,* edited by Lloyd Ulman, Barry Eichengreen, and William T. Dickens, 128–66. Brookings.

Moffitt, Robert. 1992. "Incentive Effects of the U.S. Welfare System: A Review." *Journal of Economic Literature* 30 (March): table 10.

Molle, Willem. 1990. *The Economics of European Integration: Theory, Practice, Policy.* Brookfield, Vt.: Dartmouth Publishing.

Monheit, Alan C., and Philip F. Cooper. 1993. "Health Insurance and Job Mobility: Theory and Evidence." Rockville, Md.: Agency for Health Care Policy Research.

National Center for Education Statistics. 1992. *Digest of Education Statistics, 1992.*

National Foundation for Unemployment Compensation and Workers' Compensation. 1992. *Highlights of State Unemployment Compensation Laws, January 1992.* Washington.

———. 1993. *Highlights of State Unemployment Compensation Laws, January 1993.* Washington.

Neumark, David, and William Wascher. 1992. "Employment Effects of Minimum and Subminimum Wages: Panel Data on State Minimum Wage Laws." *Industrial and Labor Relations Review* 46 (October): 82–89.

New York State Teachers' Retirement Board. 1992. *Compilation of Laws Covering New York State Teachers' Retirement System, As Amended through August 15, 1992.* Albany.

Okun, Arthur M. 1975. *Equality and Efficiency: The Big Tradeoff.* Brookings.

Olson, Craig A. 1993. "Health Insurance and Adverse Selection in the Labor Market." University of Wisconsin at Madison, Industrial Relations Research Institute.

Ontario Ministry of Treasury and Economics. Unpublished data. Ottawa.

Organization for Economic Cooperation and Development (OECD). Various years. *OECD Employment Outlook.* Paris.

Oritz Miranda, Carlos. 1993. "The North American Free Trade Agreement: Potential Migration Consequences." *Migration World* 21(1): 16–19.

Padoa-Schioppa, Fiorella. 1990. "Union Wage Setting and Taxation." *Oxford Bulletin of Economics and Statistics* 32 (May): 143–67.

Pashigian, Peter. 1980. "Has Occupational Licensing Reduced Geographic Mobility and Raised Earnings." In *Occupational Licensure and Regulation,* edited by Simon Rottenberg, 299–333. Washington: American Enterprise Institute.

Pierce, Marian. 1993. "The Temporary Agricultural Worker Program and Caribbean Sugar Cane Workers." *Migration World* 20(5): 35–36.

Rebick, Marcus. 1993. "The Japanese Approach to Finding Jobs for Older Workers." In *As the Workforce Ages: Costs, Benefits, and Policy Challenges,* edited by Olivia S. Mitchell, 103–24. Ithaca, N.Y.: ILR Press.

Reder, Melvin, and Lloyd Ulman. 1993. "Unionism and Unification." In *Labor in an Integrated Europe*, edited by Lloyd Ulman, Barry Eichengreen, and William T. Dickens, 13–44. Brookings.

"Revised Collective Redundancies Directive." 1992. *European Industrial Relations Review* 225 (October): 24–26.

Rothstein, Richard. 1993. *Setting the Standard: International Labor Rights and U.S. Trade Policy.* Briefing Paper. Washington: Economic Policy Institute.

Rottenberg, Simon, ed. 1980. *Occupational Licensure and Regulation.* Washington: American Enterprise Institute.

Ruhm, Christopher J. 1991. "Are Workers Permanently Scarred by Job Displacements?" *American Economic Review* 81 (March): 319–24.

Sala-i-Martin, Xavier, and Jeffrey Sachs. 1991. "Fiscal Federalism and Optimum Currency Areas: Evidence for Europe from the United States." Working Paper 3855. Cambridge, Mass.: National Bureau of Economic Research.

Samuelson, Paul. 1948. "International Trade and the Equalisation of Factor Prices." *Economic Journal* 58 (June): 163–84.

Sellekaerts, Brigitte H., and Stephen W. Welch. 1983. "Noncompliance with the Fair Labor Standards Act: Evidence and Policy Implications." *Labor Studies Journal* 8 (Spring): 124–36.

———. 1984. "An Econometric Analysis of Minimum Wage Noncompliance." *Industrial Relations* 23 (Spring): 244–59.

Shelburne, Robert C., and Robert W. Bednarzik. 1993. "Geographic Concentration of Trade-Sensitive Employment." *Monthly Labor Review* 116 (June): 3–13.

Smith, Robert S. 1992. "Have OSHA and Workers' Compensation Made the Workplace Safer?" In *Research Frontiers in Industrial Relations and Human Resources*, edited by David Lewin, Olivia S. Mitchell, and Peter D. Scherer, 557–86. Madison, Wis.: Industrial Relations Research Association.

"Social Charter State of Play." 1992. *European Industrial Relations Review* 227 (December): 25–31.

"Social Policy and the Maastricht Summit—Confusion Reigns." 1992. *European Industrial Relations Review* 216 (January): 2–3.

Streeck, Wolfgang. 1993. "The Rise and Decline of Neocorporatism." In *Labor in an Integrated Europe*, edited by Lloyd Ulman, Barry Eichengreen, and William T. Dickens, 80–101. Brookings.

Swaim, Paul, and Michael Podgursky. 1990. "Advance Notice and Job Search: The Value of an Early Start." *Journal of Human Resources* 25 (Spring): 147–90.

Tanzi, Vito, ed. 1982. *The Underground Economy in the United States and Abroad.* Lexington, Mass.: Lexington Books.

Teachers Insurance and Annuity Association, College Retirement and Equity Fund (TIAA-CREF). Various years. *Annual Report.*

Trejo, Stephen J. 1991. "The Effects of Overtime Pay Regulation on Worker Compensation." *American Economic Review* 81 (September): 719–41.

"Trends in Trade Union Membership." 1991. *OECD Employment Outlook, July 1991*, pp. 98–100.

"Trends in Women's Work, Education and Family Building." 1985. *Journal of Labor Economics* 3 (January, supplement).

Turner, Lowell. 1993. "Prospects for Worker Participation in Management in the Single Market." In *Labor in an Integrated Europe*, edited by Lloyd Ulman, Barry Eichengreen, and William T. Dickens, 45–79. Brookings.

"Unemployment Benefit Rules and Labour Market Policy." 1991. *OECD Employment Outlook, July 1991*, pp. 199–236.

U.S. Department of Health and Human Services. Social Security Administration. 1992. *Social Security Programs throughout the World, 1991*. September.

U.S. Department of Labor. 1993a. *Employment and Earnings* 40 (March): 82, table C-8.

———. 1993b. *Minimum Wage and Maximum Hours Standard under the Fair Labor Standards Act.*

———. 1993c. *Twenty Years of OSHA Federal Enforcement Data: A Review and Explanation of the Major Trends.*

U.S. Department of Labor. Bureau of Labor Statistics. 1990a. *International Comparisons of Hourly Compensation Costs for Production Workers in Manufacturing, 1975, 1980, and 1982–89: Supplementary Tables for BLS Report 787.* April.

———. 1990b. *International Comparison of Hourly Compensation Costs for Production Workers in Manufacturing in 1989.* Report 787. April.

U.S. Department of Labor. Unemployment Insurance Service. 1991. "The Decline in Unemployment Insurance Claims Activity in the 1980s." Occasional Paper 91–92.

U.S. General Accounting Office. 1990. *Child Labor: Increases in Detected Child Labor Violations throughout the United States.* GAO/HRD-90–116.

———. 1991. *Child Labor: Characteristics of Working Children: Briefing Report to Congressional Requesters.* GAO/HRD-91–83BR.

———. 1993. *Dislocated Workers: Worker Adjustment and Retraining Notification Act Not Meeting Its Goals.*

U.S. House of Representatives. Committee on Foreign Affairs. 1992. *Chinese Forced Labor Exports to the United States.* Hearing before the Subcommittee on Human Rights and International Organization. 102 Cong. 1 sess. Government Printing Office.

U.S. House of Representatives. Committee on Ways and Means. 1993. *1993 Green Book.* Committee Print. 103 Cong. 1 sess. Government Printing Office.

U.S. Senate. Committee on Finance. 1986. *Enforcement of U.S. Prohibitions on the Importation of Goods Produced by Convict Labor.* Hearing before the Subcommittee on International Trade. 99 Cong. 1 sess. Government Printing Office.

———. 1992. *Trade Adjustment Assistance for Dislocated Workers.* Hearing. 102 Cong. 1 sees. Government Printing Office.

Wasylenko, Michael. 1991. "Empirical Evidence on Interregional Business Location Decisions and the Role of Fiscal Incentives in Economic Development." In *Industry Location and Public Policy,* edited by Henry W. Herzog, Jr. and Alan M. Schlottman, 13–54. University of Tennessee Press.

Wessels, Walter J. 1981. *Minimum Wages, Fringe Benefits, and Working Conditions.* Washington: American Enterprise Institute.

Young, S. David. 1987. *The Rule of Experts.* Washington: CATO Institute.

Index